Praise for Patrick McKeown

"The world's leading expert on brea[...]
Mel Robbins, [...]

"The Oxygen Advantage". I had no idea how critical it is to do nasal breathing. It is amazing stuff."
Tim Ferris, entrepreneur, author, podcaster, and lifestyle guru (in an interview with David Allen)

"The Oxygen Advantage" is one of the best books that I have read this entire year . . . one of my favorite books in the world actually."
Ben Greenfield, author of the New York Times bestseller book "Beyond Training"

"The Oxygen Advantage" was a game-changing read and is one of the top books we recommend at XPT, not only for health and fitness professionals but for any individual looking to optimize the most important processes in their body."
Laird Hamilton, XPT Extreme Performance Training™

Praise for "Breathing for Yoga," by Patrick McKeown and Anastasis Tzanis:

"For the past 20 years, McKeown has researched why so many of us breathe so poorly and how we can do it better and improve our lives. He's spent several more years piecing together this carefully constructed compendium of yoga knowledge and distilling it into step-by-step directions, illustrations, scientific context, biomechanics, biochemistry, and more!"

"My advice: Take a seat, shut your mouth, breathe it in."
James Nestor, New York Times bestselling author of "Breath: The New Science of a Lost Art"

ALSO BY PATRICK MCKEOWN:

Asthma-Free Naturally

Close Your Mouth

Always Breathe Correctly

Anxiety Free: Stop Worrying and Quieten Your Mind

Sleep with Buteyko: Stop Snoring, Sleep Apnoea and Insomnia

Buteyko Meets Dr. Mew: Buteyko Method for Children and Teenagers

The Oxygen Advantage®

Atomic Focus

The Breathing Cure

Breathing for Yoga

ABOUT THE AUTHORS

PATRICK MCKEOWN is an international breathing expert and author based in Galway, Ireland. Since 2002, he has worked with thousands of clients to improve breathing, sleep, sporting performance, anxiety, panic disorder, resilience, concentration, and chronic illness. His clients include elite military special forces (SWAT), Olympic coaches and athletes.

To date, Patrick has written ten books about breathing, including "The Oxygen Advantage"—his pivotal work—which has been translated into 16 languages. His latest books are "Atomic Focus" (2021), "The Breathing Cure" (2021), and "Breathing for Yoga" (2023).

Patrick is the Founder and Director of Education for Oxygen Advantage®, which teaches breathing and focused attention for resilience and improved sports performance. He is also the Clinical Director of Buteyko Clinic International, which teaches breathing re-education and training to help address a variety of health conditions including asthma, anxiety, panic attacks, snoring, and sleep apnea.

Patrick is a Fellow of The Royal Society of Biology and a member of The Academy of Applied Myofunctional Sciences. His work has been published in "The Journal of Clinical Medicine."

Patrick is the creator of a number of patented breathing support products including MyoTape to help ensure safe nasal breathing during sleep, SportsMask to improve respiratory muscle strength, Buteyko Belt for improved functional breathing, and Nasal Dilator for easier breathing through the nose during exercise.

When asked, "What was the one thing you got from breathing training over the past twenty-four years?" Patrick has no hesitation in answering—"It transformed my life; arming me with the tools to get out of my head, focus my attention, make better decisions, sleep better, and cope better with life challenges."

Patrick's work has been featured on USA Today, CNN, the BBC, TED X, and in The New York Times, The Times (UK), and Men's Health Magazine, to name a few.

OxygenAdvantage.com; ButeykoClinic.com; MyoTape.com

ANDREW DUNNE is a certified fitness instructor, teacher, and author.

He also has a jump rope-focused YouTube channel which has helped thousands of people improve their fitness.

Followers of his channel often inquire about his breath training, wondering how he is able to speak clearly while jumping rope intensely and for long durations, yet seemingly breathing effortlessly. But this wasn't always the case.

Andrew's interest in breathing and meditative practices occurred while living in South Korea. There, he took to jumping rope, hiking, and long-distance running including ultramarathons—not only for exercise but to relax his mind. He also trained in boxing and martial arts. After a few particularly deflating sparring sessions, Andrew realized his breathing had severely compromised his performance.

That's when Andrew's research and personal experimentation into breath training intensified and led him to Patrick McKeown's book "The Oxygen Advantage."

Implementing the teachings in that book marked a turning point in Andrew's physical performance, mental health, and overall sense of well-being. Therefore, Andrew was excited to work with Patrick on this book to help increase awareness of nasal breathing and breath training.

Prior to living in Asia, Andrew attended university in Dublin where he conducted research into the relationship between body image, gender, aging, and physical activity leading to a Master of Philosophy degree. He presented this work at international academic conferences and in peer reviewed publications.

While living in South Korea, in addition to teaching at universities, Andrew regularly contributed health and fitness-oriented articles to The Korea Times and The Korea Herald.

Andrew continues to help others with their strength and conditioning through his YouTube channel and one-on-one, in addition to teaching at a local school.

MOUTH BREATHER

Shut Your Mouth:
The Self-Help Book for Breathers

BY

PATRICK McKEOWN

AND

ANDREW DUNNE

Printed in Ireland.

For information address: Patrick McKeown, Loughwell, Moycullen, Co Galway, H91H4C1, Ireland.

Email: info@oxygenadvantage.com; info@buteykoclinic.com

FIRST EDITION PUBLISHED 2024.

Publisher: OxyAt Books

ISBN: 978-1-909410-35-0

Editing by Louise McGregor and Dr. Catherine Bane

Cover design and Illustrations by Bex Burgess

Typeset by Karl Hunt Design

MOUTH-BREATHER

noun

/ˈmaʊθˌbriðər/ MOWTH-bree-dhuhr

1. *Medicine.* A person who habitually or frequently breathes through the mouth instead of the nose.

2. *North American slang.* A stupid person.

OXFORD ENGLISH DICTIONARY

"If A equals success, then the formula is:

A = X + Y + Z,

X is work.

Y is play.

Z is keep your mouth shut."

———————

ALBERT EINSTEIN

CONTENTS

INTRODUCTION

I KNOW WHAT YOU ARE THINKING ...

"What could you possibly teach me about something as fundamental as breathing? I've been doing that just fine my whole life, thanks!"

Believe me, I hear that a lot.

In our fast-paced, modern lives, many of us have unconsciously developed breathing patterns that are less than ideal. Mouth breathing is problematic because it can negatively impact sleep quality, facial development (especially in children), dental health, respiratory function, and overall health and well-being.

But it's not just about mouth breathing! Frequent sighing or yawning, audible breathing at rest, breathing faster and harder into the upper chest, snoring, or even momentary pauses in our nighttime breathing—these are all telltale signs that our breathing is less than optimal and could use some fine-tuning.

It may surprise you to learn that the way you breathe affects every system, organ, and cell in your body. It can boost your immunity, support functional movement, and enhance cognition, cardiovascular health, athletic performance, physical health, emotional well-being, craniofacial development, and sleep. Quite simply, breathing optimally can enrich your quality of life in every domain.

What would _you_ most like to get from bringing optimal breathing into your life?

You may wish to "get out of your head" and quieten a racing mind. Perhaps you'd like to promote relaxation and calm and increase sleep quality. Or perhaps you'd like to improve your physical and mental performance. If you have nasal congestion or asthma, your goal may be to reduce respiratory symptoms and be able to breathe more freely. Perhaps it's a combination of the above.

Whatever your primary motivation, finding guidance on the best way to breathe is not unlike navigating hucksters in the Wild West.

One breathing instructor advises taking a full deep breath to ventilate all regions of the lungs, to "Bring in life-giving oxygen and get rid of 'toxic' carbon dioxide." Another says, "Don't breathe too much air—this reduces blood flow and oxygen delivery throughout the body." Some instructors suggest that breathing during physical exercise should only be through the mouth, while others advise breathing in through the nose and out through the mouth, or breathing in and out through the nose.

With so many competing viewpoints, it's no wonder people are confused!

This book offers a straightforward science-backed approach to better breathing. It provides a compilation of simple yet effective exercises that you may tailor to your unique needs and goals.

To complement the book and to support you in implementing better breathing in your everyday life, a user-friendly app (OxygenAdvantage) is available for free download.

BREATHING

"IN TODAY'S CLASS, we're going to talk about gas exchange," announces Professor Jackson.

Jimmy, who sits at the back of the classroom, lets out a monstrous fart.

"How was that for gas exchange, sir?" he asks.

The classroom fills with laughter.

"Proper breathing is one of the most important factors when it comes to determining your health", replies the professor as he makes his way to the whiteboard.

Stepping away from the whiteboard, where he has written the word BREATHING in large capital letters, he grimaces, shoots Jimmy a sharp look, and opens a window.

THE FOUNDATION FOR OPTIMAL BREATHING

ALTHOUGH BREATHING IS usually an automatic bodily function, we do have the ability to control our breathing, and we can use this to our advantage. We can choose to slow down or speed up breathing, take fuller or more shallow breaths, and even hold our breath for a period of time.

Many, many functions in the body are affected directly or indirectly by breathing. Your heart rate, metabolism, circulation, immune system, and even your ability to release toxins and body fat, all rely on healthy, functional breathing.

With some awareness of our breathing patterns and the right breathing exercises, we are able to influence several major functions of the body by simply altering our breath.

If you are building the house of your dreams, the most important part to get right is the foundation. If the foundation is not strong, the house will crumble.

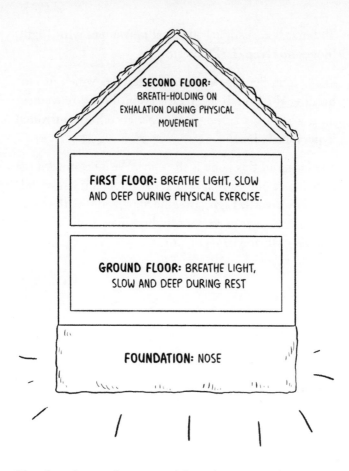

The foundation for optimal breathing is to keep your mouth shut and **breathe through your nose during rest, physical exercise, and sleep.**

The ground floor is to practice **Breathe Light, Slow, and Deep** (LSD) breathing, to train everyday breathing patterns.

The first floor is doing **physical movement with Light, Slow, and Deep** (LSD) breathing.

The second floor is the **stressor exercises** which include **holding the breath** after exhalation during movement until a strong air hunger is experienced or **controlled hyperventilation**.

The layout of this book is the same. We'll begin with the importance of breathing in and out through the nose, followed by **Breathe Light**, **Breathe Slow**, and **Breathe Deep** during rest, then movement, and capping it off is **Breath Holding During Movement**.

BREATHE IT IN

———

ASIDE FROM JUST KEEPING YOU ALIVE, optimizing your breathing can have a major impact on your life.

In today's hectic world, the importance of breathing is often forgotten about—the chronic stress of modern life has changed the way that we breathe for the worse, and many people dismiss the value of learning proper breathing techniques.

Perhaps it's because they feel that breathing is something that comes naturally, so why change it?

Or maybe they don't have time for it or view the skill as something limited for the "woo-woo" believers amongst us. They haven't dedicated the time they need to develop excellent breathing techniques that will serve to improve their health and well-being.

We breathe thousands of times a day. And anything you do that often, you should be an expert at, right? But there's still a lot most of us have yet to learn about improving our breathing techniques.

NO HOT AIR: THE SCIENCE BEHIND BREATHING

HUMANS NEED OXYGEN TO SURVIVE—that much, you already know. The good news is that, even as you are reading this, you're consuming oxygen without even thinking about it.

With every inhale, you're drawing in oxygen and allowing your body to perform its vital functions.

The main reason any animal breathes is to get oxygen into the body's cells. Oxygen is needed for aerobic respiration—the chemical process by which we get energy from the food we eat. Many people aren't aware that oxygen's vital functions in the human body depend on two other chemical compounds: carbon dioxide and nitric oxide.

The composition of inhaled and exhaled air differs in terms of oxygen and carbon dioxide content. When we breathe in, the air contains about 21% oxygen, 79% nitrogen, and only 0.04% carbon dioxide. However, exhaled breath contains approximately 16% oxygen, retains 79% nitrogen, and shows a marked increase in carbon dioxide, rising to about 4-5%.

Carbon dioxide is a gas produced by the body as a by-product of respiration. The carbon dioxide we produce is carried back to the lungs in the blood for us to breathe out *excess* carbon dioxide.

School science lessons leave many of us with the idea that carbon dioxide is a toxic waste gas and serves no function in the body. This oversimplification of the role of carbon dioxide underpins and perpetuates the common misunderstanding of breathing.

Contrary to popular belief, carbon dioxide plays a crucial role in oxygenation. Even when our blood is oxygen-rich, without sufficient carbon dioxide, our bodies struggle to utilize that oxygen effectively for energy production.

Our breathing pattern directly influences the carbon dioxide levels in our lungs and bloodstream. Interestingly, over-breathing can be counterproductive. By exhaling too much carbon dioxide, we may inadvertently hinder oxygen delivery to our cells, tissues, and organs. This highlights the delicate balance our respiratory system maintains and the importance of proper breathing techniques.

We will cover oxygen, carbon dioxide, and nitric oxide in more detail in the coming chapters.

WHEN THE INTERNET LEAVES YOU BREATHLESS

BOB IS SEARCHING THE INTERNET for information on how to breathe properly. There are 210,000,000 search results. Taking in the number of results, his breathing quickens. Is this what it means to improve your technique?

After spending a day sifting through the results, Bob is more confused than ever.

When his wife comes home, she asks him about his day.

"Some days I think it would be easier if I were a mole-rat," he tells her desolately. She wrinkles her nose in confusion and asks, with obvious concern, "a mole-rat?"

"I read that mole-rats can survive for six hours in extremely low oxygen environments and up to eighteen minutes with no oxygen at all," Bob explains. "That seems easier than whatever we have to do..."

Perhaps you're like Bob and have come to think that breathing is confusing.

SIMPLE TIPS FOR OPTIMAL BREATHING

LET'S SIMPLIFY THINGS WITH A few simple tips to save you from spending an entire day sifting through endless search results.

Breathe Nose

Breathing should be through the nose during rest and sleep, and even during many forms of exercise. Nasal breathing filters, warms, and humidifies the air you breathe, as well as promoting more efficient oxygen uptake and circulation.

Breathe Light

Taking a light, silent breath in through your nose and allowing a slow and gentle breath out triggers the body's relaxation response. Breathing light involves breathing less air into the body, which helps to improve everyday breathing patterns, increases blood circulation and oxygen delivery to the body, and reduces agitation of the mind. Believe it or not, a lot is going on when you breathe less!

Breathe Slow

Breathing slowly involves reducing your respiratory rate. This increases oxygen in the lungs allowing better gas exchange to take place, dampens the stress response and activates the relaxation response, bringing balance to body and mind.

Breathe Deep

Breathing deeply involves optimal movement of your primary breathing muscle, the diaphragm. This helps with oxygen transfer from the lungs to the blood, reduces the body's stress response, massages internal organs, assists with drainage of waste from the body, calms emotions, and stabilizes the spine.

Each of these exercises is accessible and helps improve your everyday breathing, bringing many benefits which we will explore fully in subsequent chapters.

Descriptions and guidance for all of the recommended exercises are included at the end of the book on page 188.

If your everyday breathing pattern is a little faster, heavier, or located in the upper chest—your body is telling the brain that there is some threat to the body. A rule of thumb is that if you can hear your breathing during rest, or have easily noticeable movements of your body as you breathe—your breathing is under par. The same goes for when you are working on your phone or computer and unconsciously stop breathing.

If you practice breathing techniques that involve taking faster, fuller breaths (controlled hyperventilation), you activate the body's stress response. If you stop breathing during rest or physical movement until you feel a strong need to breathe (simulate altitude training), you activate the body's stress response.

These techniques can cause positive adaptations to your body. Each of these exercises is at opposite ends of the spectrum—as one slightly increases oxygen and decreases carbon dioxide; while the other lowers blood oxygen saturation and increases carbon dioxide. Although not for everyone (the induced stress may simply be too much, particularly for those with chronic health conditions) these practices can be very positive.

If you are in good health, controlled hyperventilation helps cause a mental reset, releasing tension and trauma, quietening the mind, and generating a sensation of empowerment.

Holding the breath following an exhalation during movement opens the airways, increases blood flow and oxygen delivery to the brain, creates a controlled dose of psychological stress (air hunger), and causes the body to adapt to better tolerate the demands of intense physical exercise.

Techniques such as controlled hyperventilation can benefit certain individuals. However, for those beginning their breathwork journey and wishing to restore and promote healthy breathing—forget about the attention-grabbing sexy stuff you may see on social media for a while and start with the basics.

Taking a soft, silent breath in through your nose and allowing a slow and gentle breath out triggers the body's relaxation response. Breathing light, slow and deep tells the brain that the body is safe.

Breathing properly is like the case of Goldilocks and the porridge.

As we'll explore in this book, throughout the day and night, your inhalations and exhalations should not be too fast or too slow, too large or too small, but just right.

Breathing should almost exclusively be through your nose—even though initially this might seem difficult, as many of us have made a habit of breathing through our mouths. This book is not only about learning new things—it is a guide to unlearning bad habits that we have picked up.

Breaking into a bear family's house is entirely optional, but not encouraged!

BODY OXYGEN LEVEL TEST

YOU WILL KNOW YOU ARE making progress on your breathing journey when your Body Oxygen Level Test score (BOLT) is improving. You can take this simple breath-hold test by following the instructions on page 81. Each time your BOLT score improves by five seconds, your everyday breathing patterns are improving, and you are achieving the above goals of easier breathing, better sleep, improved focus and concentration, and staying calm under pressure.

If, on the other hand, you are practicing a particular breathing technique, and instead of your BOLT score improving, it lowers—this indicates that your everyday breathing pattern is getting worse. The exercises that are more likely to cause a drop in your BOLT score involve mouth breathing, faster breathing, and taking bigger breaths. Even slowing down breathing can result in a worsening of your breathing patterns if the volume of air that you draw into your lungs is too much.

Taking a big breath might be the worst thing for you to do!

The concept of a "deep breath" is often misinterpreted as a "big breath," but there's a crucial distinction. "Deep" in this context refers to the lower regions of the lungs, not the volume of air inhaled. The word deep means "far from the top." A genuine deep breath involves drawing air into the bottom portions of the lungs, rather than filling them to capacity.

When we breathe deeply, the diaphragm—our primary breathing muscle—descends, creating space for air to enter the lungs. This action causes a subtle expansion in the abdomen, sides, and back. It's important to note that this doesn't mean inhaling a larger quantity of air.

Consider a cat's natural breathing pattern as an example. While lounging by the fireplace, a cat isn't deliberately taking large, full breaths. Instead, it's naturally breathing deeply and efficiently.

Regularly taking big breaths can have counterproductive effects. This practice can lead to a decrease in carbon dioxide levels within the lungs and blood. As a result, blood flow may be reduced, compromising oxygen delivery throughout the body.

PICK YOUR MOMENT—NOT YOUR NOSE!

KIMBERLY HAD BEEN DOING HER job diligently for three years, so she decided she would ask her boss for a raise in salary. "It's about time I got one!" she said to herself.

Her boss tells her to stop by his office at 4 pm.

Earlier that afternoon, Kimberly saw that her boss's breathing was particularly noticeable. He was breathing faster than normal and breathing into his upper chest, not to mention sighing a lot.

The average person tends to breathe this way due to stress, but this way of breathing also causes a person to be stressed—it's a vicious circle. When the person is stressed, the brain is more concerned with survival and it is not a time for planning or making decisions. Asking the boss for a wage rise at this time would be like a red rag to a bull.

CAN YOU WAIT TO FILE MY REQUEST FOR TIME OFF ON TUESDAY?
WHY WAIT UNTIL THEN?
THAT'S WHEN THE BOSS STARTS THE DAY WITH YOGA SESSIONS!

A longtime yoga practitioner, Kimberly quickly decides it is not the ideal day to discuss the subject with her boss—a wise decision.

The next time you see someone who you think looks agitated or unwell, observe their breathing. It will tend to be noticeable, often in the upper chest, and faster than normal.

The perfect breather looks as if they do not breathe at all.

At rest, it is difficult to see the breathing of a healthy person. Their breathing is in and out through the nose, silent, regular, slow, and deep.

DON'T FORGET— THE NOSE KNOWS BEST!

AFTER RETURNING HOME FROM SCHOOL, Vivian asked her son Richard to tell her two things he learned that day.

"In history class, we learned about ancient Egypt and a king named Tutankhamun. In math class, we learned that $(a+b)^2 = a^2 + b^2 + 2ab$". "Is it okay if I use my computer now?" he shoots back impatiently.

"Just a moment, sweetie," Vivian replies. "First, we need to talk about something."

"Is it about what happened in science class?" asks Richard, a furrow appearing on his brow. "Mom, I'm sorry about bringing your baking soda to school, but I wanted to show my friends how to make a volcano."

She raises her eyebrows. "We'll get to that," she replies,

making a mental note to give her son a volcano-centric talking to.

"Richard, your principal phoned. He said you were not concentrating in most of your classes, and you were disrupting your teachers."

We want our children to be good students, to score well on their exams, and to thrive academically and socially so they can achieve their life goals. But are we providing the education necessary to help achieve this?

While he could recite poetry and facts about the periodic table, in his ten years of formal education thus far, Richard has not been taught how to breathe for better concentration and stress management.

Imagine having to devote twelve years to formal education where concentration is a must-have, but not providing kids with the tools to concentrate. Sounds ridiculous, right?!

The importance of learning how to breathe properly from a young age cannot be overemphasized. Poor breathing habits lead to reduced sleep quality and a lack of blood supply and oxygen to the brain, which can subsequently lead to hyperactivity, agitation, slow thinking, and decreased information retention.[1],[2]

1 Bonuck, K., Freeman, K., Chervin, R. D., & Xu, L. (2012). Sleep-disordered breathing in a population-based cohort: behavioral outcomes at 4 and 7 years. *Pediatrics*, 129(4), e857-e865.
2 McKeown, P. (2021). The Breathing Cure: Exercises to Develop New Breathing Habits for a Healthier, Happier and Longer Life: OxyAT Books.

Research demonstrates that people with normal nasal function, who are able to easily breathe through their noses as nature intended, have improved cognitive function and energy levels in comparison to people with chronic nasal issues.[3] People who cannot breathe efficiently through their noses due to nasal congestion have demonstrated significantly more cognitive dysfunction, fatigue, and slower reaction times on computerized testing.

3   Soler, Z. M., Eckert, M. A., Storck, K., & Schlosser, R. J. (2015, November). Cognitive function in chronic rhinosinusitis: a controlled clinical study. In *International Forum of Allergy & Rhinology* (Vol. 5, No. 11, pp. 1010-1017).

RYANAIR VULTURES

HIGH-FLYING BIRDS SUCH AS the vulture can soar at over thirty thousand feet. To put this in context, a Ryanair jet travels at an altitude of thirty-five thousand feet. But describing Ryanair and vultures in the same sentence might be a tad unfair to the vulture—at least the vulture doesn't make you fly with your knees around your ears!

To ensure adequate oxygen at altitude, the birds have air sacs close to their rear ends—which then transfer air to their lungs.[4] When the next breath is drawn into the body, stale air is moved from the lungs to the air sacs for release into the atmosphere.

We humans, however, rely on our noses to breathe properly. Let's talk about how that works, and why exactly the term "mouth-breather" might be even more of an insult than you originally thought!

---

4   https://carnegiemnh.org/how-birds-breathe-with-their-butts/

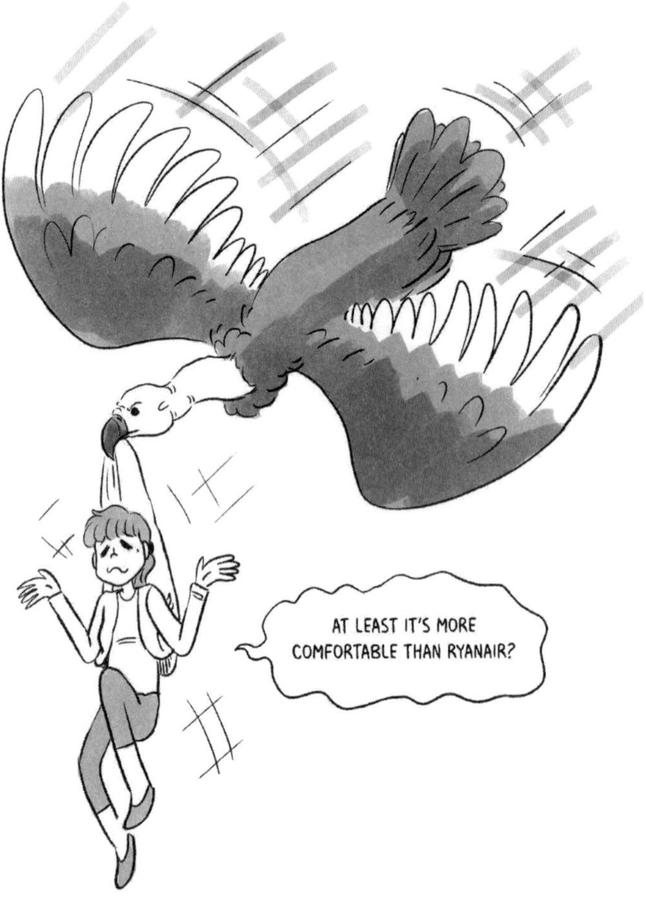
AT LEAST IT'S MORE COMFORTABLE THAN RYANAIR?

BREATHE NOSE

"It's not the size of the nose that matters,
it's what's inside that counts."

STEVE MARTIN

THE MOUTH IS SIMPLY NOT designed for breathing.

Don't believe me? Look inside your mouth.

You're most likely going to see some combination of your teeth, gums, tongue, hard palate, soft palate, and throat. Do any of these body parts serve any purpose for breathing other than letting air into the body and down your throat? To put it crudely, your mouth is a hole (no sniggering at the back!).

It doesn't take a rocket scientist to realize that the mouth is for eating, drinking, talking, and, if you play your cards right, kissing.

Your nose does everything when it comes to breathing. Your mouth does virtually nothing.

Even during most forms of physical exercise, it doesn't make sense to breathe through the mouth. Your nose naturally opens up to allow more airflow during physical exercise[5]—further proof that it should be used during running and other strenuous activities.

5 Hasegawa, M., & Kern, E. B. (1978). The effect of breath holding, hyperventilation, and exercise on nasal resistance. *Rhinology*, *16*(4), 243-249.

SHUT YOUR MOUTH AND LISTEN!

BRIAN EXCITEDLY FILLS HIS DAD in on everything he's learned at school that day, leaning on the kitchen table, his homework spread out in front of him.

"I learned that all mammals at rest breathe in and out through their noses," he explains, a tiny scholar lecturing on his chosen subject.

"Human babies breathe through their noses at rest, too. One of the primary functions of the nose is breathing. But in our culture, countless people breathe with their mouths. However, our mouths are designed for things like eating, drinking, and talking—not breathing. . ."

Brian trails off as he notices his dad's mind drifting away. His dad blinks, and turns to him, an apologetic expression on his face.

"Sorry, son, what did you say? I wasn't listening . . ."

"I was just about to tell you what ears are for" said an annoyed Brian.

Had his dad paid attention to Brian, he may have learned some valuable information.

Brian is right. When humans are born, we are obligate nose breathers. We are genetically programmed to nose breathe. However, many children, often unbeknownst to them, shift to mouth breathing during childhood.

Perhaps it's a case of a stuffy nose, and "monkey see, monkey do". Children observe others breathing with their mouths and emulate this pattern. They haven't just picked it up off the grass.

BREATHE FREELY

AS A DAD, JOHN SUFFERED TERRIBLY from a stuffy nose. And while he could breathe through it, when he did, he felt that he was not getting enough air. Without even thinking about it, he just switched to breathing through his mouth as it was less uncomfortable.

At a recent gathering of former classmates, John chatted with Lauren who had embarked on teaching people how to improve their breathing. When the topic of having a stuffy nose came up, Lauren explained that the nose could be decongested in just a few minutes by simply holding the breath.

In the middle of the gathering, John could be seen breathing out gently through his nose, holding his nose with his fingers to stop breathing, and nodding his head up and down ten to fifteen times. After twelve head nods, John let go and breathed in through his nose. He repeated the exercise five times, with about a one-minute rest between each. His nose felt less congested and his breathing felt much freer after the five head-nodding bouts. John had by now captured the attention of the room.

Lauren further explained to John, that even if he felt a little uncomfortable breathing through the nose—to continue to do so. The more the nose is used for breathing, the easier it gets.

THE INNER GAME OF GOLF

DURING A RECENT INTERVIEW, international golfer Rory McIlroy shared that he had a rib issue for years, and is convinced it was because he was not breathing properly.[6] By training to breathe using his diaphragm (rather than from his chest), his rib issue resolved. Rory also knows that breathing the right way helps the nervous system to be more responsive. Furthermore, he explained that he used to have allergies, but since breathing through his nose and not his mouth, his allergies have gone— because the nose can filter the pollen and microbes and the mouth can't.

I agree when Rory says,

"Things like this . . . are so simple that people just don't realize".

---

6   https://www.youtube.com/watch?v=yitj9nKS43g

Breathing through the nose engages the diaphragm and does all the things that Rory explained above. I hope he is using MyoTape during sleep. That will help ensure nasal breathing throughout the night and help him wake up feeling much more refreshed.

It's an occupational hazard for a golfer to have nasal allergies to pollen and grass. No avoiding that one for Rory, unless he improves his BOLT score to over 25 seconds and learns to decongest his nose by simply holding his breath. This would allow him to breathe through his nose throughout the day and night and during those all-important golf competitions.

In a recent game, Rory was taking a high-stakes shot. The commentator intuitively says, "Rory needs to breathe." But *how* should he breathe?

How one breathes in the weeks leading up to competition is important. By bringing optimal breathing practice into everyday life, one has the tools to draw upon when they are needed most.

As Rory sizes up to take the putt, his objective should be to put his critical thinking mind aside and slow the speed of his breathing, which will lower the speed of his heartbeat. This allows all energy to be devoted to taking the putt. By taking a soft breath in through the nose, and allowing a slow relaxed breath out, attention is shifted from the mind and into the body. Slowing the breath and engaging the diaphragm by nasal breathing stimulate the vagus nerve, bringing down the speed of the heartbeat. When the brain interprets that the body is safe, all energy can be placed on taking the putt.

Yes, it's the simple things in sports that matter.

A JAW-DROPPING TALE

FIFTY YEARS AGO, Dr. Egil Peter Harvold, a Norwegian dentist who later moved to America, recognized that children with stuffy noses had crooked teeth. To investigate this, he blocked the noses of young monkeys with nose plugs to force them to breathe through an open mouth.[7] With the monkeys' noses blocked, it only took a few months before their faces and jaws changed in comparison to the monkeys who were allowed to breathe normally.

The end result was not pretty. As the monkeys' jaws were set back, their faces became longer and their teeth crooked.

When I talk about Harvold's study on monkeys, people are aghast. I agree—it was cruelty to animals.

Yet millions of children are persistently breathing through an open mouth, and hardly anyone bats an eyelid. What about the cruelty to children?!

---

7 Tomer, B. S., & Harvold, E. P. (1982). Primate experiments on mandibular growth direction. *American journal of orthodontics, 82*(2), 114-119.

Whether you nose-breathe or mouth-breathe has a large impact on jaw, dental, and facial development.[8] Despite what every toddler around you might think, the nose isn't just for picking, but rather it performs as many as thirty important functions in the human body. We cover many of these in the coming pages. Please also see page 85 for a summary.

8   Lin, L., Zhao, T., Qin, D., Hua, F., & He, H. (2022). The impact of mouth breathing on dentofacial development: A concise review. Frontiers in public health, 10, 929165.

NITRIC OXIDE— YOUR PERSONAL AIR STERILIZER

BRANDON READ A SCIENTIFIC PAPER that said that nose breathing and humming increase the release of a gas called nitric oxide which helps open the airways. Humming increases nitric oxide in the nose fifteenfold.[9]

The nasal cavity releases nitric oxide and it is inhaled through the nose. Thanks to nitric oxide, oxygen absorption in the body can be increased by as much as 10%[10] simply by nose breathing. On the other hand, the mouth does not release nitric oxide, and no nitric oxide is inhaled through the mouth, resulting in less oxygen absorption.

---

9 Weitzberg, E., & Lundberg, J. O. (2002). Humming greatly increases nasal nitric oxide. *American journal of respiratory and critical care medicine, 166*(2), 144-145.

10 Lundberg, J. O. N., Settergren, G., Gelinder, S., Lundberg, J. M., Alving, K., & Weitzberg, E. (1996). Inhalation of nasally derived nitric oxide modulates pulmonary function in humans. *Acta physiologica scandinavica, 158*(4), 343-347.

As a breath is taken in through the nose, nitric oxide is released and it follows that airflow down into the lungs, where it redistributes blood throughout the lungs, increasing blood flow by as much as 24% in the upper areas of the body.[11]

Nitric oxide has also been found to play a role in maintaining healthy lung function. It sterilizes inhaled air, supporting your immune system. This may help to reduce infection of the sinuses, throat, airways, or lungs by inactivating viruses and bacteria.[12] Higher levels of nitric oxide are associated with a decrease in certain respiratory infections and fewer cold symptoms.

Interestingly, some scientists believe that the human nose may have utilized nitric oxide when humans made the transition to bipedal or upright mammals.[13] Standing upright would have negatively affected blood and oxygen supply to the upper areas of the lungs and body. Breathing through the nose to harness nitric oxide would have helped counteract this problem by redistributing blood throughout the lungs.

---

11 Sánchez Crespo, A., Hallberg, J., Lundberg, J. O., Lindahl, S. G., Jacobsson, H., Weitzberg, E., & Nyrén, S. (2010). Nasal nitric oxide and regulation of human pulmonary blood flow in the upright position. *Journal of applied physiology, 108*(1), 181-188.

12 De Groote, M. A., & Fang, F. C. (1995). NO inhibitions: antimicrobial properties of nitric oxide. Clinical Infectious Diseases, 21(Supplement_2), S162-S165.

13 Sánchez Crespo, A., Hallberg, J., Lundberg, J. O., Lindahl, S. G., Jacobsson, H., Weitzberg, E., & Nyrén, S. (2010). Nasal nitric oxide and regulation of human pulmonary blood flow in the upright position. *Journal of applied physiology, 108*(1), 181-188.

Brandon makes a vow to himself to hum his way through life to increase his nitric oxide levels. Brandon's teammates get a little irritated with his humming after a while. He soon earns the nickname "the human refrigerator".

But, with his newfound nitric oxide levels, he doesn't mind. Humming helps him calm down.

He takes a soft breath in through his nose and hums with a slow relaxed exhalation. Humming slows down the speed of the exhalation allowing for more oxygen to be absorbed. It also stimulates the vagus nerve, helping the body and mind to relax even further. The vagus nerve runs from the brain through the face and chest to the belly. It helps control the body's parasympathetic nervous system, sometimes called the relaxation or "rest and digest" response.

Unlike the body's sympathetic nervous system, which helps your body respond to dangerous or stressful situations by heightening mental awareness and speeding up your heart rate, the parasympathetic nervous system slows down your heart rate, thereby creating a calmer state and a sense of relaxation.

Being quite competitive, Brandon relishes in the knowledge that his teammates are getting upset while he is becoming calmer. A competition in calmness is one he knows he can win.

WHAT YOUR NOSE KNOWS

RUSSELL AND BRITTANY ARE just about to clean the dishes after saying goodbye to their dinner guests when they notice their son sniffing the couch where their friends had exchanged pleasantries and anecdotes throughout the evening.

"Eugene, stop doing that. Get over here. We need your help with the dishes," Russell tells him, as Brittany stares on in confusion.

Is their son some kind of cat who makes judgments on people via scent? Should she take him to a doctor . . . or a vet?

You may have observed kids performing this behavior —sniffing the area or object someone used. Indeed, you yourself may have smelled a seat or an object after someone used it when you were younger. While this may seem peculiar, the sense of smell is important in learning about others and choosing both human and animal mates.

Studies have found that we use signals picked up via smell, otherwise fancily referred to as olfaction, in helping us choose friends, associates, and even life partners.[14]

14 Ihara, Y., Aoki, K., Tokunaga, K., Takahashi, K., & Juji, T. (2000). HLA and human mate choice: tests on Japanese couples. *Anthropological Science, 108*(2), 199-214.

SNIFFING OUT MR. RIGHT

LET'S TURN OUR ATTENTION to what (for some) is the eternal question: what do women find attractive in a man?

Facial appearance and brawn are important. A decent bank balance can also help. I once heard my mother-in-law say, "When poverty comes in the door, love flies out of the window"—cynical, but she might have had a point.

In case I forget to mention it, thanks very much for purchasing this book!

But, for example, could it be the sexy scent emanating from a man that is the deciding factor for a potential mate? No, I'm not just talking about his aftershave.

There is an interesting phenomenon that applies to both human and animal mate choice. Based on the sense of smell, women typically choose men who are genetically dissimilar to themselves—an important trait developed across centuries of evolution to ensure that relatives didn't mate with each other. If you are dying to know, this is called the major histocompatibility complex (MHC).

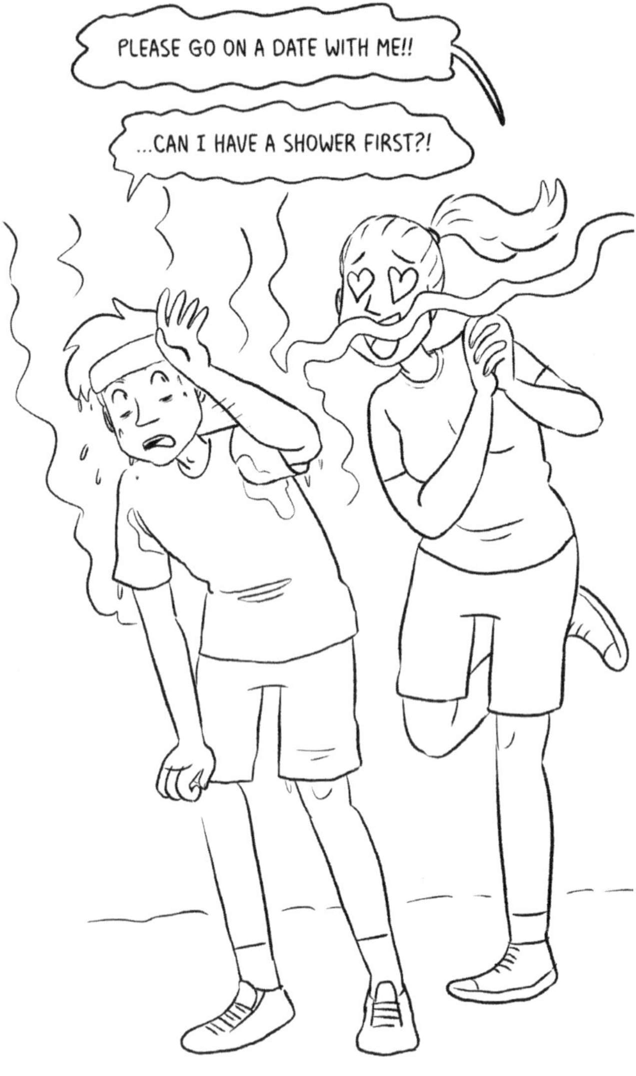
PLEASE GO ON A DATE WITH ME!!
...CAN I HAVE A SHOWER FIRST?!

When a woman is taking the contraceptive pill, her body is in a hormonally pregnant state and she is more likely to choose a man with similar MHC genes to herself.[15] When pregnant, there is no desire for her to seek out a mate. But there is a desire for her to be close to family for help with rearing the baby.

Couples with dissimilar MHC genes are more satisfied and faithful to each other—opposites do, in fact, attract, though perhaps not in the way most romcoms would try to convince you they do.

15   Roberts, S. C., Gosling, L. M., Carter, V., & Petrie, M. (2008). MHC-correlated odour preferences in humans and the use of oral contraceptives. *Proceedings. Biological sciences, 275*(1652), 2715–2722.

Conversely, couples with matching genes show less satisfaction with each other and are more likely to have wandering eyes.

Now, I bet that has got you thinking as different scenarios play in your mind. What happens if a woman meets a male partner while she is not on the pill, and then goes on the pill or vice versa? Does she, all of a sudden, feel less drawn to her chosen partner?

In any event, back to breathing—influencing choice of partner is just another wonderful function of the nose!

TRUST YOUR NOSE

EVERY SUNDAY, DANIEL CLEANS his house from top to bottom. He even vacuums the curtains.

"It's like a chemical factory in here," his friend Leonard remarks as he glances around the spotless house on a visit that Sunday afternoon.

"I'm just trying to protect myself against germs," Daniel shoots back, hurriedly sweeping the floor where Leonard walks.

"That's what your nose is for," Leonard points out. "Unlike your mouth, your nose acts as a filter catching tiny particles before they can get into your lungs and therefore, it helps protect you from germs, bacteria, and other pollutants."

"And what about the pollutants you're bringing in on your shoes?" Daniel asks. Leonard sighs and kicks them off.

"Happy now?"

"Happier," Daniel replies, scrubbing the door handle with a rag.

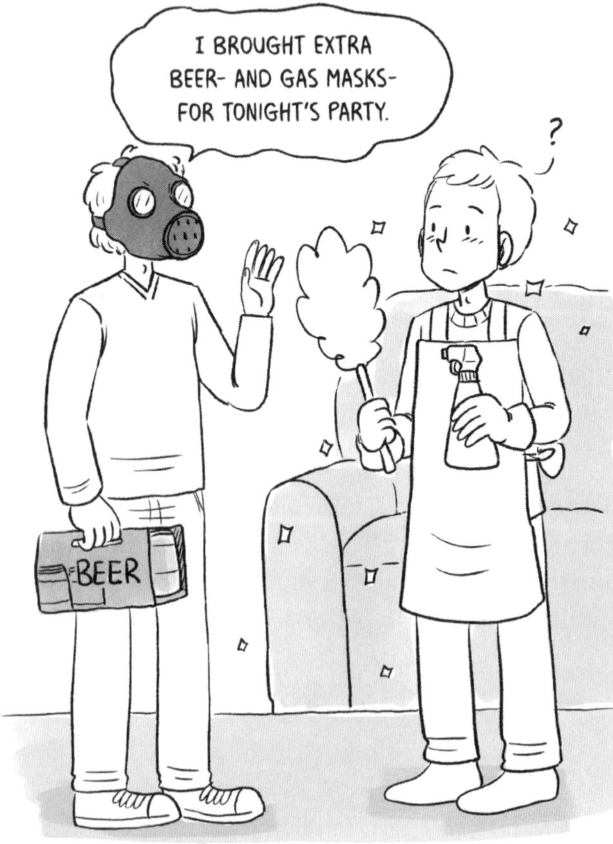
I BROUGHT EXTRA
BEER- AND GAS MASKS-
FOR TONIGHT'S PARTY.
?
BEER

NOSE BREATHING NATIVES

OLIVIA AND HER TEAM OF SCIENTISTS are traveling the globe in search of hunter-gatherer tribes—hoping to learn about their lifestyles and share the newfound knowledge with the world.

The team of scientists observed that in cultures that still live in their native ways, people breathe in and out through their noses. Olivia, much to her surprise, earns the nickname "Venus Flytrap" amongst the tribesmen in Papua New Guinea, apparently because her mouth is always hanging open.

Mouth breathing generally involves breathing a larger volume of air than your body needs. *Overbreathing* in this way is considered a disease state and contributes to a huge range of common physical and mental health problems, including insomnia, sleep apnea, cardiovascular disease, sexual dysfunction, headaches, back pain, brain fog, PMS, nasal congestion . . . the list goes on.[16]

---

16 McKeown, P. (2021). The Breathing Cure: Exercises to Develop New Breathing Habits for a Healthier, Happier and Longer Life: OxyAT Books.

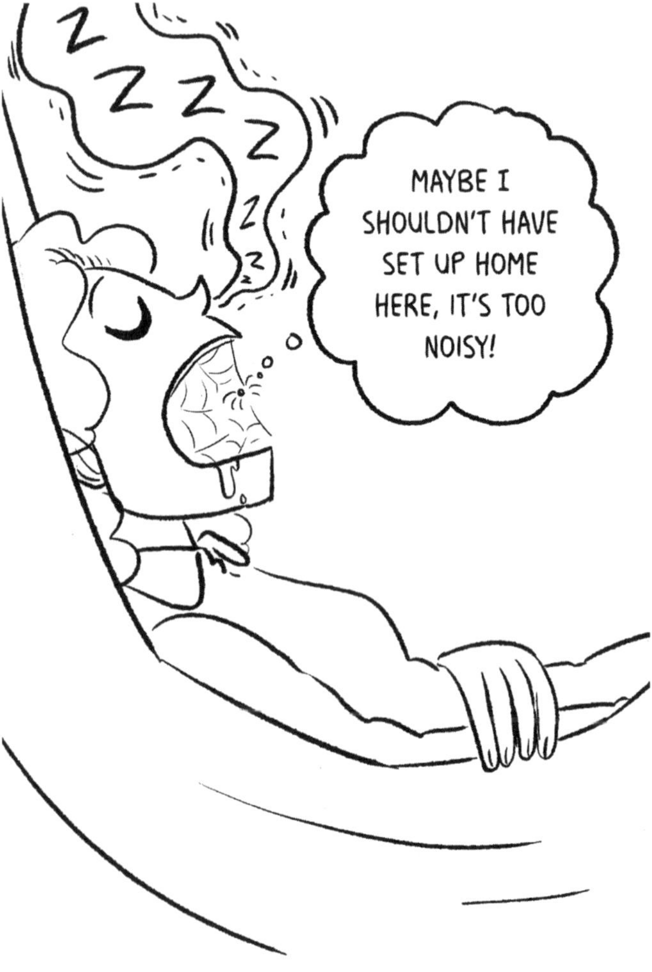
ZZZZZZ
MAYBE I SHOULDN'T HAVE SET UP HOME HERE, IT'S TOO NOISY!

In the modern world, working long hours indoors with artificial light, rushing from task to task, sleeping poorly, eating processed foods, and living sedentary lives that negatively affect posture have become the norm. These lifestyle patterns send stress signals to our bodies that affect how we breathe.

Unless you consciously practice breathing through the nose, these daily stresses can cause mouth breathing, fast breathing, and upper chest breathing, which stimulate the body's stress response (sometimes called the "fight or flight" response).

A CHILLING TALE OF MOUTH BREATHING

VINCENT RECENTLY STARTED A NEW JOB at a butcher's shop. Slipping on his short-sleeved shirt and new name tag, he is ready to join the crew. His main duty involves selling meat to customers and, when their well-stocked counters run low, ducking into the freezer to pull out new products.

The freezer is set at minus 18 degrees Celsius, whereas the butcher shop remained at a comfortable 19 degrees. Only one problem—Vincent can't understand how his colleagues regulate their body temperature and resist the cold of the freezer so well. He would always put on a sweatshirt when he had to retrieve something from the freezer. Then, when he returned to the main shop floor, he felt too warm. Were his colleagues hardier stock than he was? More used to the shock of the cold and then the comparatively balmy heat of the shop floor?

Every time Vincent made his way to the freezer, he would pull in a few big breaths through his mouth and let them out again, to watch the cool air pool into condensation in front of him, followed by a few chilly coughs.

Little did he realize that the cold air was irritating his throat, drying out his mucus membranes, and causing him to cough. Unbeknownst to Vincent, he continues mouth breathing after exiting the freezer. This is not ideal.

Unlike the mouth, the nose plays a vital role in thermoregulation—the body's ability to maintain its core temperature within a specific range.[17] The nasal passages are filled with blood vessels that warm the incoming air, helping to regulate our body temperature.

WE NEED TO MOVE VINCENT TO GET TO THE SAUSAGES.

---

17   Widdicombe, J. (1997). Microvascular anatomy of the nose. Allergy, 52, (40 Suppl):7-11.

A BREATH OF FRESH AIR

MEGAN IS TEASED AND BULLIED by classmates because of her bad breath. Sometimes, when students check their watches or look up at the clock when Megan is in the area, rather than saying "tic-tock", they say "Tic Tac, Tic Tac".

Megan wants to tell them all to shut their mouths, but she knows she has to first practice what she preaches. She presses her lips together and hopes her toxic cloud of breath won't reach her classmates.

Her dentist refers her to a periodontist, who, upon first meeting Megan notices she has cracked lips. The gum disease specialist treats the bacteria and plaque that are causing inflammation around her gums. Furthermore, the periodontist points out to Megan that she suffers from dry mouth which can result in bad breath.

"Have you always been a mouth breather?" she asks Megan. Megan frowns at her in confusion. It sounds like an insult.

"I'm not sure" she admits. "Am I a mouth breather?"

No dentist has ever spoken with Megan about breathing, so she was unaware that her breathing could affect the smell of her breath.

The periodontist politely educates Megan that the mouth has two main functions, eating and speaking, while breathing is one of the primary functions of the nose, especially when at rest.

Megan does her best to take it in. She's shocked to learn that mouth breathing can cause crooked teeth, another one of her issues, as well as lead to inflamed tonsils, cavities, and it can even negatively affect the shape and development of the face and jaw.[18]

A person's tongue should rest against the roof of the mouth, applying gentle outward pressure which causes the teeth to shape around the tongue in a healthy arch form. However, if you mouth breathe, the tongue cannot rest on the roof of the mouth. This results in an underdeveloped, narrow top jaw which can cause a narrower facial structure, facial asymmetry, and overcrowded teeth.

Since Megan had learned that many children have straight teeth when they are toddlers, she quickly went through family photo albums, only to notice that her now-crowded teeth were once straight, much to her surprise.

18 Triana, B.E., Ali, A.H., & León, I.B. (2016). Mouth breathing and its relationship to some oral and medical conditions: physiopathological mechanisms involved. https://api.semanticscholar.org/CorpusID:37727955

During childhood and adolescence, Megan developed the habit of leaving her mouth open and breathing through her mouth. Her parents also breathed the same way, unconsciously modeling the behavior that would lead to issues later in life.

THE SECRET TO SUCCESS— SYMMETRY AND NASAL BREATHING

STUDIES HAVE FOUND THAT ALMOST everyone displays affinities to faces that are attractive, even babies. For instance, research shows that infants, as young as two months old, show a preference for attractive faces. That is to say, babies look longer at photos of attractive faces; in these studies, attractiveness was evaluated by adults who rated photos of human faces on a spectrum from attractive to unattractive.[19] This suggests that standards of, and preferences for, attractive faces are either innate or acquired much earlier than previously supposed.

---

19 Langlois, J. H., Roggman, L. A., Casey, R. J., Ritter, J. M., Rieser-Danner, L. A., & Jenkins, V. Y. (1987). Infant preferences for attractive faces: Rudiments of a stereotype?. Developmental psychology, 23(3), 363.

But attractiveness is an individual preference, right? Well, yes, but a key component of measurable facial attractiveness is symmetry.

Since mouth breathing can lead to facial asymmetry, unless children are instructed to nose breathe, they could suffer in terms of dental development and facial attractiveness and even success in their careers. There is evidence that in their work and careers, unattractive people meet prejudices in hiring, advancement, and salary. There's a reason the term "mouth-breather" is used as an insult!

How wide is the distance between your cheeks, relative to the distance between your brow and upper lip?

In terms of evolution, men with wider faces were more likely to reproduce and become successful in securing scarce resources from other men, to support themselves and their offspring.[20]

---

20 Haselhuhn, M. P., Wong, E. M., Ormiston, M. E., Inesi, M. E., & Galinsky, A. D. (2014). Negotiating face-to-face: Men's facial structure predicts negotiation performance. *The Leadership Quarterly, 25*(5), 835-845.

Men with wider faces earn more money, as they are better at negotiating.[21] In a study of the top five hundred companies in the United States, **CEOs with wider faces generally oversaw stronger financial performance at companies**.[22] A wider face indicates higher levels of testosterone, which correlates to greater success in high-stress professional environments.

As a narrow-faced, former mouth breather, I am happy to report that not everything goes their way. Men with wider faces are more likely to cheat in order to increase financial gain and to act immorally at work.

The moral of the story is to breathe through your nose with your tongue in the correct resting posture from child-hood—and, if you're a parent, it's important to model that behavior for your children to help ensure the best outcomes for them later in life.

21 https://www.eurekalert.org/news-releases/720389
22 https://www.sciencedaily.com/releases/2011/08/110825152503.htm

TAKE MY BREATH AWAY

A GROUP OF MEN ARE ATTENDING a seminar with their partners to learn how to become better kissers.

"Be careful about biting someone's lip when you kiss," warns the instructor. "Some people find it painful. Others enjoy it but don't overdo it or apply too much pressure. Nobody wants a bloody valentine."

After a half-hour of smooching study, the attendees are already starting to feel more confident in their intimate prowess. However, there are two final points to address: breathlessness and excessive drooling.

"Consider yourself lucky if your partner takes your breath away," the instructor jokes. "But if you are having trouble breathing when you kiss, you likely breathe through your mouth. You can't breathe through the mouth and kiss with the mouth at the same time. Fortunately, the solution is easy. Breathe through your nose while kissing."

There is a slightly uncomfortable shuffle in the room; it's clear there are more than a few mouth-breathers in here.

DATE NIGHT ESSENTIALS

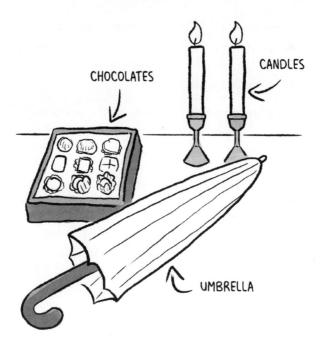

CHOCOLATES

CANDLES

UMBRELLA

"Breathing through your nose can also help reduce how much of your saliva lands on your partner's chin and face. Breathing through the mouth can result in the mouth opening unnecessarily wide while kissing, causing the release of saliva. Nose breathing can help avoid this problem," the instructor continues before a hand shoots up at the back of the room. She nods for the man to ask his question.

"Isn't drooling a sign of passion?" the man asks. Beside him, his partner rolls her eyes skywards—a sure sign of her feelings towards his excess saliva. "How do you know if you're producing too much saliva?"

"Easy," the instructor replies, shooting his partner an apologetic look. "If your partner asks for a tissue or needs an umbrella, that's a good indication that you are drooling too much."

But kissing isn't the only intimate practice that can impact your breathing—sexual intercourse, too, can have a major influence on how your breathing functions. If it's good, that is! An orgasm can serve to help clear the nose, whether alone or with a partner—though you may want to keep the pinched nose and head-nodding to a minimum if you're trying to get lucky!

FOLLOW YOUR NOSE TO STEER YOU TO SUCCESS

SHANNON IS WORRIED AHEAD OF her driving test after a night of ruminating on her failed driving test one month ago where she accidentally turned on the radio when she should have turned on the windshield wipers. On the way to the test center, she finds her thoughts sluggish and her mind blocked. So she drives to the nearest café and orders a large coffee with an extra shot of espresso—enough caffeine to rouse a tranquilized elephant from its slumber.

Thirty minutes later though, her thinking is still slow, and, as her test draws nearer, she can't help but worry about reaching for the wrong knob all over again.

Just then, however, she remembers the results of a study she had read in science class which found that inhaling through the nose can improve mental focus.

The nose is in constant communication with the brain through the olfactory nerve which is located in the upper inside part of the nose. The olfactory nerve is responsible for our sense of smell, but it also improves visuospatial function which is necessary to identify and process visual information about where objects are in space.[23]

Individuals with a high level of visuospatial intelligence tend to have an affinity for skills such as drawing, painting, sculpting, navigation, map reading, architecture, and archery.

Visuospatial function may have evolved hundreds of thousands of years ago when humans were hunter-gatherers. A high level of visuospatial intelligence helped primitive humans find food, explore new territories, scan environments for predators, and literally sniff out danger.

The ability to catch prey and avoid becoming prey is no longer such a necessity. However, that does not mean that visuospatial function is not important. For example, impaired visuospatial ability makes it more challenging to judge distances, and therefore tasks like driving and walking without bumping into objects become more difficult.

So, it seems there is some truth behind the expression "You have a good nose (for something)." The expression is used

---

23 Perl, O., Ravia, A., Rubinson, M. *et al.* Human non-olfactory cognition phase-locked with inhalation. *Nat Hum Behav* **3**, 501–512 (2019).

to pay someone a compliment—not about their sense of smell, but rather their almost natural ability to find and recognize something.

A SNIFF DOWN MEMORY LANE

ALEXIS HAS AGREED TO TAKE PART in a study connected with sensory deprivation.

Under the watchful eyes of the white coats clustered around a central table, she's asked to close her eyes and perform various tasks to assess hand-eye coordination.

Next, the teams of scientists investigate her sense of smell.

On the table in front of Alexis were several objects and scents that she had to smell and then report whether they aroused any mental or emotional responses. Not exactly how she thought she'd be spending her afternoon, but, in the name of science, she begins to sniff.

She soon begins to form connections between smell and memory—more vividly than she could have imagined. When presented with the scent of pine, she immediately recalls family summer camping trips in the woods during her childhood, while the scent of chalk aroused negative emotions related to an incident in primary school where she felt a teacher had unfairly singled her out for misbehaving.

She's only slightly embarrassed to admit that the scent emanating from a smelly sock brought her a sense of comfort, as she was certain it belonged to her husband.

Research demonstrates that sense of smell plays a pivotal role in shaping our behavior, memory, and emotional responses by activating parts of the brain called the amygdala and the hippocampus.[24]

---

24 Kadohisa, M. (2013). Effects of odor on emotion, with implications. *Frontiers in Systems Neuroscience, 7*, 66.

A SCENT-SATIONAL LESSON

"AWESOME! MOM HAS MADE a fresh batch of cookies," Jamie says aloud, inhaling deeply as the sweet scent of dessert wafts through the house. His school bag is still slung over one shoulder, and his mom lifts a hand to stop him in his tracks before he snatches up a handful of cookies.

"Not so fast," she warns him. "Before you eat a cookie, I want you to open your gym bag."

Reluctantly, he pulls it open, and the thick fog of sweat and staleness fills the air. He wrinkles his nose apologetically.

"Sorry, Mom. I forgot to wash my soccer uniform after practice."

"Now, that's a yellow card if I've ever seen one," she shoots back, a hand over her nose.

As a science teacher, Jamie's mom always makes use of such situations as educational opportunities.

"Because of your nose, you were able to smell the freshly

baked cookies and your dirty clothes. One of the main roles of the nose is the sense of smell. The nose has over four hundred receptors that detect and process odors. But did you know that our sense of smell has many vital roles?" she asks him.

"No," Jamie responds, stealing another hopeful look at the cookies. "Like what?"

"Well, every time you or your father hasn't showered, I hold my breath," jokes his mother. "Seriously, though, through our sense of smell, our brains learn about our environments. Our sense of smell checks the quality of the air and substances we breathe. It helps keep us safe. For example, our sense of smell helps us detect smoke before we see a fire, or it can warn us to avoid food that has spoiled. Our brains learn to make associations with certain smells."

"Anything else?" Jamie asks. The cookies, he thinks to himself, don't look spoiled to him. His nose is telling him that much.

"Our sense of smell is also used to test for traumatic brain injury. Impaired ability to smell can indicate neurological damage."[25]

"I thought my nose was just for picking!" Jamie shoots back. "Now can I have a cookie?"

---

25 Ruff, R. L., Riechers, R. G., Wang, X. F., Piero, T., & Ruff, S. S. (2012). A case–control study examining whether neurological deficits and PTSD in combat veterans are related to episodes of mild TBI. *BMJ open, 2*(2), e000312.

"I don't know why I bother trying to teach you," she laughs and pushes the plate towards him.

"Just one more thing: your nose also plays a part in your sense of taste. If it weren't for your nose, you couldn't properly taste your food or drinks. The nose communicates with the orbitofrontal cortex, a part of the brain responsible for taste perception."

"The orbito-what?" Jamie asks through a mouthful of cookie, spraying crumbs everywhere. His mom hands him a napkin as she continues.

"The pairing of tastes and smells is what enhances the flavors of the foods and beverages we consume, making them much more appetizing.[26] And that is why, when your sense of smell is impaired due to a common cold or other condition, it affects your ability to perceive flavors, resulting in a less flavorful experience."

"Very cool!" replies Jamie, eyeing another cookie already.

"Yes. Go ahead and take a bite of one of the cookies and notice how it tastes. Then pinch your nose and take another bite," she instructs him, never missing the opportunity to teach. Experimentally, he does as he's told, and nods as he chews down another bite.

"You're right! I never realized how lucky I am to have a nose."

---

26 Rolls, E. T. (2015). Taste, olfactory, and food reward value processing in the brain. *Progress in neurobiology*, 127, 64-90.

TACKLING MOUTH BREATHING

IT IS THE FIRST PRACTICE OF the winter rugby season. Given the cooler temperatures, the coach advised all players to nose breathe as much as possible, something which they've been incorporating into their training sessions.

"Look around, lads, many of you are hunched over gasping for air," he announces, as he guides the scrum around him. "Many of you are still breathing through your mouths. In essence, it is not about the volume of air taken into the lungs. What's more important is how much oxygen transfers from the lungs to the blood and the blood to the working muscles. The body utilizes oxygen better when breathing is in and out through the nose."

The coach continued, "The more you practice breathing through the nose, the easier it will become. Practice when you are resting at home, doing light-to-moderate physical exercise, and over time, you'll notice it becomes easier to do when training."

Sam, known to his teammates as "Bear" on account of his size and large amount of body hair, interrupts. "Coach, what if you have lots of nose hair—is that bad for nose breathing?"

Eyeing Sam's generous nasal hair, the coach assures him swiftly. "Great question, Sam. If you have more nose hair than normal, it can be trimmed slightly. But those nose hairs serve an important purpose. They trap foreign objects and large particles like dust and dirt."

"Foreign objects? Sam has so much nose hair, his nostrils could sub in for goalie," teases one of his teammates.

In addition to hair, the nose is lined with a thin moist layer of tissue called a mucous membrane. As the name might suggest, this membrane makes mucus, commonly referred to as "snot." The mucous membrane not only adds moisture and heat to the air we breathe in, but its mucus captures and prevents dust, germs, and other small irritants from reaching the lungs.

"Bless you," one player says as another player sneezes.

"You can thank your nose for that sneeze," the coach interjects. "Sneezing is how your nose gets rid of unwelcome particles that are captured in its hairs or mucus."

"So, sneezing can help us remain healthy?" the team captain asks, leaning forward with interest. It's flu season, after all, and it seems like everyone on the team has been passing the same bug back and forth for so long.

"It can indeed."

"Coach, I have one more question about nose breathing," he adds enthusiastically.

"Well, you're particularly nosey today, aren't you?" jokes the coach. "What's your question?"

"If the nose acts as a filter that captures particles before they can enter our lungs, can nose breathing help prevent allergic reactions like hay fever and pollen allergies?"

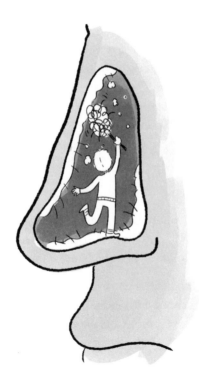

"Yes. The nose plays a crucial role in controlling hay fever and pollen.[27] Great question! Now, lads, let's get back to training".

"Hey, coach!"

"Yes, Bear?"

"Forget it. I'll mind my own Bees-ness."

"Very funny, Bear. Now buzz off."

---

27 Petruson, B., & Theman, K. (1996). Reduced nocturnal asthma by improved nasal breathing. *Acta oto-laryngologica*, *116*(3), 490-492.

A NOSE FOR MEALTIME MANNERS

"TAKE YOUR TIME, CHERYL. There's no rush and there's extra food in the oven," Cheryl's mother assures her, as Cheryl shovels away another mouthful of food.

All at once, it gets caught at the back of her throat, sending her into a sputtering coughing fit.

This kind of incident happens more often than Cheryl would like, earning her the family nickname "Hoover" since she always vacuums down her food—and is only marginally quieter.

But that was not the issue. Cheryl doesn't take big mouthfuls, nor does she eat fast. She adequately chews her food before swallowing.

The cause of these regular occurrences of choking and coughing when eating and drinking is a combination of mouth breathing and talking while she had food in her mouth.

Recall that two of the main functions of the mouth are eating and speaking. But that does not mean the two should occur at the same time. And not just because it's bad manners!

VRRRRRRR

Speaking while you have food in your mouth can lead to problems swallowing. If you are a mouth breather, you may be at a greater risk of choking and coughing at mealtimes.

When food is swallowed, it moves from the mouth down into the throat and then into the stomach through a tube called the esophagus.

The throat is a part of the respiratory system responsible for breathing. When you breathe, air moves into the throat. From there, the air passes into the lungs through the primary airway known as the trachea. At the top of the trachea is a flap of tissue called the epiglottis that prevents food and liquids from entering the trachea when swallowing. However, talking, drinking, and mouth breathing while you have food or liquid in your mouth increases the likelihood of the food or liquid entering the trachea and causing choking and coughing.

The relationship between issues with swallowing and mouth breathing points to the importance of breathing through the nose. Breathing through the nose can reduce the risk of complications when swallowing food, not to mention spraying your dinner partners with most of your meal in the process!

TAKE THE BODY OXYGEN LEVEL TEST

"HE BEAT ME AGAIN," Joel complains to Master C.

"But you are the better, more skillful fighter," he points out.

"Then why does he keep beating me?" asks Joel.

"Did you hear how Greg was breathing?" replies Master C.

"I could barely hear him breathing. It was as if he wasn't breathing at all..."

"Exactly, Joel. Less is more."

"I don't understand," replies Joel, his nose wrinkling with confusion.

"You need to rest. Come back tomorrow and I will teach you more..."

Master C enters the karate dojo the next day to find Joel already there practicing. But practicing his moves isn't going to get him where he wants to go.

"You won't beat an opponent if you are breathing poorly throughout the day. When breathing is slightly faster and harder during rest, it will be faster and harder during physical exercise, and you are more likely to 'gas out.' Poor breathing throughout the day doesn't automatically correct itself during physical activity," Master C explains, as Joel throws punches and swings kicks.

"Huh?" Joel pants, glancing around at his master.

> "Let's do the Body Oxygen Level Test (BOLT). This simple test of how long you can comfortably hold your breath provides feedback on how much air you need during rest and physical exercise. To do the test, exhale normally through your nose. Pinch your nose with your fingers to stop breathing. Time how long you can hold your breath for and still have normal breathing when you resume breathing. In other words, it is not the maximum length of time that you can hold your breath."

"Try it now, and don't worry about what you get. It is just to provide feedback on your breathing patterns."[28]

---

28 Kiesel, K., Rhodes, T., Mueller, J., Waninger, A., & Butler, R. (2017). Development of a screening protocol to identify individuals with dysfunctional breathing. *International journal of sports physical therapy, 12*(5), 774.

Joel followed the BOLT instructions, holding his breath, then letting go at 14 seconds—this is when he had the *first definite desire or need to breathe.* Master C explains that if the BOLT score is less than 25 seconds, you are more likely to breathe fast, hard, and into the upper chest.

"Efficiency applies to breathing just like anything else. It is about achieving maximum productivity with minimal wasted effort. Your BOLT score indicates how efficiently you are breathing."

"The first step to becoming an efficient fighting athletic machine is to reach a BOLT score of 25 seconds or more. For professional athletes, the goal is to achieve a BOLT score of at least 40 seconds. Your breathing improves every time your BOLT score increases by 5 seconds."

But, as Master C points out to Joel, "Breathing through the nose isn't the only thing that matters. It's *how* you breathe through the nose that can make a major difference. Let's get into light breathing, and how it improves your performance and focus."

Please note the BOLT is only suitable for adults as it doesn't provide much feedback for assessing children's breathing. For a complete free children's breathing program, refer to the ButeykoClinic App or MyoTape.com

FUNCTIONS OF THE NOSE

THE HUMAN NOSE HAS a minimum of 30 functions, many of which we discuss in detail in this book. Here is a summary of what your nose does for you:

- **Filtration:** The nose acts as a filter, trapping dust, allergens, and other particles in the mucus and nasal hair to prevent them from entering the lungs.

- **Temperature regulation:** The nose warms inhaled air to body temperature before it reaches the lungs.

- **Humidification:** The nose adds moisture to inhaled air, which is important to reduce inflammation and maintain proper lung function.

- **Sense of smell (olfaction):** The nose contains olfactory receptors that allow us to detect and identify various odors.

- **Taste perception:** The nose communicates with a part of the brain responsible for taste perception called the orbitofrontal cortex. This brain center receives taste and smell signals and processes them together, coupling smell and taste.

- **Defense mechanism:** The nose is part of the body's defense system against harmful particles and pathogens. The mucus membrane traps potentially dangerous substances. The nose produces nitric oxide, which plays a role in maintaining healthy lung function and may help to protect against certain respiratory infections.

- **Memory:** The sense of smell is closely linked to memory formation and recall.

- **Speech and phonetics:** The nose plays a role in how we sound when speaking.

- **Helps to induce relaxation:** Nasal breathing provides resistance to slow down the breathing rate. The nasal passages are smaller than the mouth, which means that air has to pass through them more slowly. This creates a natural resistance that helps to regulate breathing rate and promote relaxation.[29]

- **Increases oxygen uptake in the blood:** Nose breathing is more effective at increasing oxygen uptake than breathing through the mouth.

- **Improves cognitive function:** Persons with normal function of the nose have improved cognitive function

---

29 Russo MA, Santarelli DM, O'Rourke D. The physiological effects of slow breathing in the healthy human. Breathe (Sheff). 2017;13(4):298-309. doi:10.1183/20734735.009817

and energy levels in comparison to persons with chronic nasal issues.

- **Promotes better sleep:** The nose is necessary for proper nasal breathing, which has been shown to contribute to deeper and more restful sleep.

BREATHE LIGHT

MASTER C INSTRUCTS JOEL to return in two weeks. In the meantime, he tells him to "Breathe light through his nose at all times."

"This involves breathing less air for periods of time during the day to retrain your breathing patterns so that you need less air during physical movement. Sit down and place your attention on your breathing. Take a soft breath of air into your nose, almost as if you are hardly breathing, and allow a relaxed and slow gentle breath out."

"By breathing less air into your lungs, carbon dioxide increases a little in the body and you will feel that you are not getting enough air. This is good feedback that you are doing the exercise correctly."

While you are practicing, remember to leave some air for other people in the room. Don't be so greedy with your breathing!" he explains.

"With practice, your BOLT score will increase. This tells you that your breathing pattern has improved, and your breathing will be more efficient during rest and physical exercise."

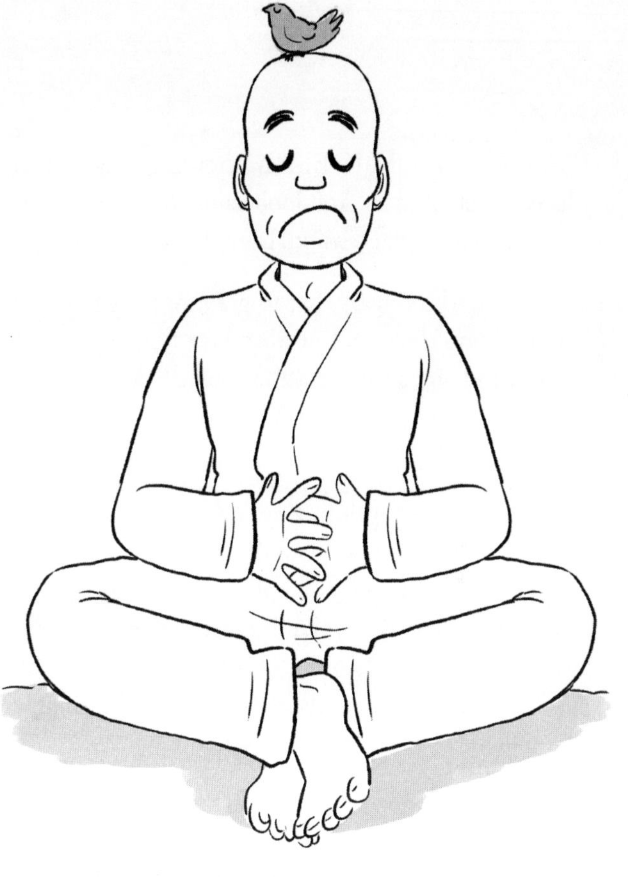

BREATHE EASY

"WELCOME BACK, JOEL," Master C greets Joel with a smile, two weeks later. "You look calm. You used to come into my dojo with facial tension. Light breathing suits you."

"I have been told for years that to get more oxygen and to get rid of carbon dioxide, I need to take big, deep breaths in and out, and since my mouth is a bigger hole, I usually used it for breathing," Joel admits sheepishly. Master C shakes his head.

"A common misconception. But carbon dioxide is not a waste gas. You see, your body contains a protein called hemoglobin which is contained in red blood cells. Hemoglobin is responsible for carrying oxygen. The key to releasing oxygen from red blood cells to your muscles, tissues, and brain is to increase carbon dioxide levels in your body. That happens when you *don't* take big breaths in and out."

He continued, "Although this effect was discovered back in 1904 and is included in most, if not all, medical textbooks that have a section on respiratory physiology, it remains a secret even to many breathing instructors. If you would like to find out a little more about this, Google *Bohr effect*."

"I see. Breathing light through the nose consistently increases your mental faculties, as we can clearly see with someone like you, Sensei."

"Very good, Joel. But remember, 'brown nosing' doesn't have nearly as much cognitive benefit," Master C teases him lightly.

DIGESTING THE IMPORTANCE OF LIGHT BREATHING

LESLIE IS COMPLAINING TO HER friend about feeling uneasy and is dealing with a plethora of physical niggles too.

"Feel how cold my hands are!" she exclaims, planting them against Pamela's arms. "And my lips are always dry. And I feel like I can't eat anything without upsetting my stomach!"

Pamela, who has just returned from a seminar on breathing in America, learned first-hand that such symptoms could be the result of breathing poorly.

"What if I told you that you could help these issues simply by changing your breathing habits?" suggests Pamela.

"I'd probably have cold feet about the idea," Leslie shoots back, giggling.

"Go on, I'm serious," urges Pamela. "Just try it for a few minutes. You have nothing to lose except your issues. And you have plenty of them..."

"Fine. What should I do?" asks Leslie.

Pamela gives just two simple instructions: "One, take a shorter breath in than what you feel you need. And two, allow a very slow, relaxed, gentle breath out. All should be through the nose and as silent as possible."

Breathing through the nose while slowing down and softening your breathing will reduce the volume of air you breathe and generate a slight sensation of *air hunger*. While this may sound like a bad thing, "under-breathing" for a few minutes improves blood circulation, increases oxygen delivery, and helps with recovery.

Leslie can't believe what's happening. After only a few minutes of practicing this breathing pattern, the temperature of her hands is increasing and there is more saliva in her mouth. On top of that, she feels a warm sense of relaxation—almost sleepiness.

Pamela grins proudly, then adds: "If you make a habit of breathing more gently, I think you will digest food better, too. When the body feels safe, it is ready to digest food. "Over-breathing" and breathing too fast heightens the body's stress response which is the opposite of what you want to allow you to properly digest food."

"Neato!" shoots back a delighted Leslie. "Thanks, Pam."

"I guess lunch is on you today. How about some largemouth bass?!" responds Pamela playfully.

"Too soon, Pam," Leslie replies with a grin.

FROM STRESS TO SUCCESS

THE DAY OF PATRICK'S COLLEGE exam has arrived. The subject: economics. Unfortunately, he isn't so economical with his breathing.

Patrick glances up at the clock on the wall. Seeing that his exam would start in just fifteen minutes, he feels his nerves begin to creep up. To calm his senses, he heads outside for a short walk.

Having read in a book about yoga breathing that taking full, big breaths was useful for stress relief and concentration, on his walk, he focuses on breathing with his mouth to fill his lungs with air. However, after a minute of breathing like this, he feels lightheaded and dizzy.

That lightheaded feeling continues after his walk, stretching on for several minutes into the exam. Little does he know that the full big breaths reduced oxygen delivery to his brain.

Okay, I'm going to be honest—that Patrick, panicking about an economics exam, was me. So, how should I have breathed to optimize my mental clarity?

Well, if I were to prepare for an exam today, light and slow nose breathing would be in my arsenal.

Breathing in and out through the nose would bring about improved blood flow to the brain and would help me to sleep more deeply at nighttime. The time spent studying would then generate a much better return. Back then, while my eyes were directed to the page, my attention was not. I would get to the end of the page, not having the foggiest idea of what I had just read.

It took a lot of work for me to achieve academically. Children with mouth breathing have lower academic achievement and poorer working memory than those who nose breathe.[30] Sleep issues are more common in those who mouth breathe. Children who have sleeping issues have almost ten times the risk of learning difficulties.[31]

While a certain amount of stress is good and keeps us alert, too much stress is a bad thing for our physical and mental health. The brain is continually spying on our breathing, even during sleep. When we breathe a little faster, harder, or upper chest, the brain interprets that the body is under threat, and launches us into a "fight or flight" response to

30 Kuroishi, R. C. S., Garcia, R. B., Valera, F. C. P., Anselmo-Lima, W. T., & Fukuda, M. T. H. (2014). Deficits in working memory, reading comprehension and arithmetic skills in children with mouth breathing syndrome: analytical cross-sectional study. *Sao Paulo Medical Journal*, *133*, 78-83.

31 Triana, B. E. G., Ali, A. H., & León, I. G. (2016). Mouth breathing and its relationship to some oral and medical conditions: physiopathological mechanisms involved. *Revista Habanera de Ciencias Médicas*, *15*(2), 200-212.

protect the body. That's not the ideal scenario to experience while heading into an exam.

So, knowing what I now know about breathing, what would I have done to manage the stress during this exam?

Fifteen minutes prior to the exam, I would have sat down to breathe slowly, taking a soft breath in through the nose and allowing a relaxing and slow breath out, for ten minutes. The objective would be to breathe softly, to the point of feeling a tolerable air hunger. Doing this tells the brain that the body is safe and helps to conserve energy that might otherwise be spent trying to soothe the nervous system. Then, if I was feeling a little too sleepy following the exercise, I could go for a brisk walk for a few minutes, breathing in and out through the nose, to lift my energy again before starting the exam.

Simple as that.

The most important factor in staying focused under pressure is to have optimal everyday breathing patterns. Breathing through the nose during rest, sleep and exercise is a great option to improve sleep and concentration.

If you're looking for specific guidance on preparing for an exam, I have a guided audio available on YouTube or Spotify which can be found by searching: "Patrick McKeown exam preparation."

THE SIMPLICITY OF BREATH

SINCE SHE HAS BEEN UNDER a lot of stress lately with work and raising her children, Janice accepts an invite from Madison to visit her apartment for a meditative breathing session.

As soon as Janice enters Madison's apartment, she begins coughing, overwhelmed by smoke and the scent coming from the burning of several incense sticks.

"You look so tense," Madison tells her. "Take a seat on this meditation mat and cushion while I prepare the other items for our session."

Madison returned wearing the distinctive yellow robes of a Buddhist monk, carrying a box containing chakra bracelets, necklaces, and stones, as well as a mantra-carved singing bowl and prayer beads decorated with lotus plants.

"Here, put these on," Madison orders, handing Janice a pair of yoga sandals. Janice cocks an eyebrow but does as she's told. Not exactly the most stylish, but she's not here to look good, right?

"Now grab that end," Madison tells her, extending an odd-looking plant in her direction.

"What's this?" asks Janice, frowning in confusion.

"It's bamboo hedging. We'll surround this area with it to create our space of tranquility."

"What have I gotten myself into?" Janice thinks to herself, doing her best to arrange her features in a neutral fashion.

"Now, take a seat and repeat after me," instructs Madison confidently. "Ommmmmm, ommmmmm, ommmmm. . ."

"Is she about to take flight?" Janice asks herself. "And does she expect me to make those noises too?"

If, like Janice, you find the above a bit too woo-woo, rest assured that you do not require a particular setting or a special outfit and accessories to attain a sense of calm.

While you may certainly feel and look wonderfully serene in a beautiful lotus pose, breathing doesn't require formal practice. Your breath is your friend, always there for you whenever you need it. As you go about your daily activities, take note—how are you breathing?

It's more important that you regularly check in on your breathing, rather than portraying an image of serenity.

There is no spectacle. Nothing to see—this is the beauty of it.

In fact, the less bodily movement during breathing the better. When you practice breathing light, imagine that someone is observing your breathing. Your goal is to breathe so softly that the other person can hardly see you breathe.

A BREATH OF CALM

THROUGHOUT THE DAY, spend a few seconds with your attention on your breath. Here and there, whenever you have a spare moment. When waiting in line at the bank, or for the photocopier to warm up, or for the kettle to boil. The number of times that you bring your attention to your breathing is more important than the amount of time spent during one sitting.

Observing your breath helps bring solace to the mind, freeing you from being consumed with thinking. You cannot think and have your attention on the breath at the same time.

When your attention is on the breath, you are in the present moment. You are not thinking about the past or anxious about the future. Your attention is here, now.

If you are feeling stressed, take even slower, softer breaths in and relaxed, slow breaths out. This will send a signal to your brain and body that you are safe, bringing down your heart rate and activating the body's "rest and digest" response. That's all the brain cares about—survival. The brain is comfortable in the knowledge that the body is safe. Reach out and tell the brain that it's got nothing to fear at different times during the day.

How you breathe throughout the day is more important than how you breathe during a single yoga or meditation session.

"When you own your breath, nobody can steal your peace"

UNKNOWN

TAKE A BREATHER

HAROLD HAS LONG SUFFERED FROM digestive issues. His doctor diagnosed him with chronic irritable bowel syndrome.

Harold has tried several medications, in addition to changing his diet, avoiding gluten, and consuming probiotics, with little success. Eventually, after a particularly uncomfortable day trip with his friend, the friend recommends a traditional Chinese medicine practitioner.

While inquiring about Harold's history of digestive issues, the doctor learns that Harold is often under a lot of stress (not just from his malfunctioning bowels) and that Harold breathes with his mouth and into his upper chest.

"Life doesn't have to be a bowel-holding contest. The solution to your problem may be as simple as taking soft breaths in and out through your nose," the doctor tells him. Harold stares at him, unable to keep the incredulity off his face.

"I don't believe it," responds Harold. "After all, I have been told to take a deep breath when I am stressed, and I use my mouth because that's what I've seen others do."

"Well, to understand about breathing and stress, ask yourself, how do you breathe when you are feeling stressed?" calmly retorts the doctor. "Do you breathe through your mouth or nose? Do you breathe harder or lighter? Do you breathe faster or slower? Do you breathe into your chest with your shoulders moving upwards or into your belly? Do you stop breathing, sigh more, or have irregular breathing? Does your breathing feel uncomfortable?"

"When I'm stressed, I breathe faster, louder, and I often yawn and struggle to catch my breath" Harold admits after a brief pause, practically proving the doctor's point.

"In order to activate your body's 'rest and digest' processes, you must breathe in a manner that signals you are safe. The way you breathe is triggering a stress response that prepares your body to flee or fight," the doctor explains, leaning back in his seat.

"You are stimulating your sympathetic nervous system which speeds up your heart rate and delivers blood away from your stomach to areas of your body such as your muscles and brain that need more oxygen to help you escape danger. However, blood flow to your stomach is vital for proper digestion. Also, when you are breathing in a gentle, relaxed manner, you will tend to feel increased saliva in your mouth, which aids in digestion."

"I see," mutters Harold. Has it really always been that easy?" he then asks.

"To bring the body and mind into relaxation, you need to breathe the opposite way to how you breathe during stress. This means breathing through your nose, in a lighter, slower, and regular manner into your belly. Developing this habit should help improve your digestion and eliminate or at least lessen the severity of your irritable bowel syndrome," continues the doctor.

While social media might portray life as always going to plan, wishes always granted, and cash always pouring in, the reality is somewhat different. It is the nature of life that we face challenges, and it is the challenges we face that give us an appreciation when things do go our way, when we do get a lucky break.

Facing a challenge could cause you to breathe harder, faster, irregularly, into your upper chest, and typically through your mouth, ultimately leading you to feel uncomfortable. You might also find your mouth goes dry meaning there is less saliva to help digestion.

To help prevent or minimize feeling stressed, you must develop the habit of breathing gently through your nose while at rest and in the midst of tension.

"Before you leave my office, it's important that I reassure you that everyone experiences stress and as a result, may occasionally experience diarrhea. You are not alone and you have a lot of positive things going for you, Harold."

BREATHE EASY, SPEAK FREELY

LAWRENCE DEVELOPED A STUTTER as a child. Unfortunately, his stuttering persisted into adulthood.

He's a successful computer programmer, an avid photographer, and a guitarist with an intelligent, beautiful wife and two kids. Still, his stuttering affects his self-image and self-confidence.

Since his grandfather stuttered his entire life, Lawrence believes that is also his fate.

Lawrence often works alone or in an office with the same few people. This is a comfortable working environment and he stutters far less often around these people.

The same is true when he's with his wife and children. However, during large social gatherings or company meetings, where the atmosphere is often tense, Lawrence has a tough time speaking and attempts to limit interactions and communication.

Not only do tense and emotional environments cause Lawrence to stutter more often, but when he stutters it leads to further anxiety, which causes even more stuttering and anxiety. It is a vicious circle.

Unbeknownst to Lawrence, anxiety and heightened emotion affect his breathing, causing him to breathe faster and shallower. He also regularly experiences breathless moments.

Speaking is connected to breathing. We breathe in, and the air we breathe out works together with an organ at the top of the neck known as the larynx, commonly called the voice box, to produce sound.

Poor breathing can result in a lack of air to support speech. Without sufficient air, not only does speaking become more difficult, but it also results in feelings of tension. If there is tension in any area of the mouth, including the tongue or throat, stuttering can occur.

For his birthday, Lawrence's wife gets him VIP tickets to a comedy club, where he would have the chance to meet his favorite comedian backstage. During their one-on-one conversation, Lawrence is shocked to find out that the comedian used to have a terrible stutter. The well-known comedian books Lawrence an appointment with both her therapist and her speech and language specialist.

Lawrence learned breathing techniques to quieten the negative voice in his head and cope with his anxiety, to help with stuttering.

"I'm taking you out on the town tonight," Lawrence tells his wife, a few weeks after his first appointment, a bouquet of flowers in hand.

"Wow, really?" his wife asks, her eyes widening.

"Did I stutter?!" Lawrence shoots back with a devilish grin.

His wife's breathing might have picked up at the sound of her husband's flirtation—but, in general, slow breathing is the best way to manage your oxygen consumption and optimize your breathing. Let's get into it!

THIS IS THE SAME COMEDIAN WE SAW LAST WEEK? I GUESS THE STAMMER WAS A PART OF THE ACT BEFORE.

BREATHE SLOW

THE TORTOISE, WHO CAN REACH the ripe old age of 300 years, breathes only 4 times per minute. The elephant also breathes about 4 to 5 breaths per minute and has a life span of 50 to 70 years.[32]

A dog takes about 40 to 50 breaths per minute. The mouse, who lives for about 2 years, breathes 255 times per minute.

Adult humans breathe somewhere in the middle of this scale—between the tortoise and dog, at about 12 to 14 breaths per minute. A mouth breather will breathe faster than a nose breather.

Those of you who are breathing through your noses and receiving adequate oxygen to the brain may catch my drift—that our lives are not just measured by the number of our years, but also by the number of our breaths.

If that's true, then slow breathing is the best approach—but you don't need to take my word for it.

Let's get into how slow breathing can impact your day-to-day life and benefit your mental and physical health.

---

32 https://www.huffpost.com/entry/breathe-less-live-longer_b_422923

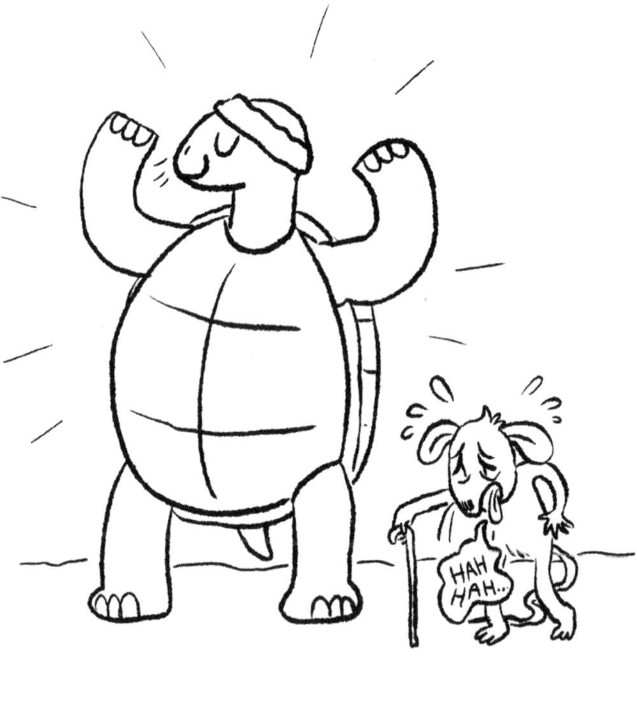
HAH
HAH...

PAWS AND TAKE A BREATH

HAVING OVERSLEPT, JANE LEFT HER house late to take her kids to school. Leaving her house later than usual meant traffic was unusually bad this Wednesday morning.

To quench her thirst in the car, she reaches into her bag for her bottle of water. However, she had been in such a hurry to leave home that she forgot to pack both her water and food for the day.

"What's next?" she mutters to herself, annoyed.

Just then, another driver changes lanes abruptly forcing Jane to slam on the brakes to avoid a collision.

"What a jerk!" Jane exclaims. "It sure is a dog-eat-dog world."

The irony is that Jane's kids and their dog are fast asleep in the backseat, blissfully unaware of what's unfolding. Even her canine companion doesn't think as much about dogs eating as she does!

Meanwhile—unlike her car which was stuck in traffic—Jane's breathing has sped up and her mind is in high gear. She tries to calm herself by various means—listening to classical music, whistling, saying positive affirmations out loud, and slowing down her breathing.

But no matter how much she tries to quieten her mind, it seems impossible, which only makes her feel even worse. Jane is caught in a vicious cycle, with literally and figuratively nowhere to go.

"If the quality of my sleep was better, I may not have overslept," she curses herself.

What she doesn't realize is that she can improve her sleep quality. She sleeps with her mouth open and also tends to mouth breathe during the day.

Unlike nose breathing, mouth breathing decreases blood flow to the brain and does not activate the body's relaxation response.

Jane attempts to bring her body and mind into balance in the car by slowing down her breathing. But, oftentimes, attempts to achieve peace of mind or mindfulness don't work when you need them most.

The key is to breathe properly at all times, which naturally makes the mind quieter and calmer and therefore helps prevent activating the body's stress response in the first place, by increasing blood flow and oxygen delivery to the brain and throughout the body. An oxygenated brain is a calm, focused brain.

Jane knows it's time to look inside and call off the dogs. Her anger and stress are not worth jeopardizing the safety of her family for.

To slow down a racing, agitated mind and therefore induce relaxation, one should hold one's breath after a normal exhalation for a few seconds. Exhale gently through the nose. Pinch your nose with your fingers to stop breathing for 5 seconds or so. Resume breathing in and out through the nose for 10 to 15 seconds. Repeat the breath hold for 5 seconds or so. Continue with this exercise for about 10 minutes.

The next time you have a racing mind, forget about trying to meditate. How is it possible to meditate when the mind is "all over the place?"

Instead, simply hold your breath, count, and provide a singular focus.

Breathing slowly can have considerable physiological effects on the mind and body, impacting mood, heart rate, respiratory rate, blood pressure, digestion, concentration, energy levels, and sleep.

Slow, diaphragmatic breathing stimulates the vagus nerve, the main nerve of the parasympathetic nervous system (associated with the "rest and digest" state and feeling calmer and more relaxed). The vagus nerve controls organ functions such as digestion, heart rate, respiratory rate, perspiration, and muscle sensations.

A review of multiple research studies has shown that slow breathing can result in increased comfort, relaxation, pleasantness, vigor, and alertness, and reduced symptoms of arousal, anxiety, depression, and anger.[33]

During times of stress, and at bedtime, slow down your heart rate and your racing mind with soft, quiet breaths in through the nose followed by gentle, relaxed breaths out through the nose.

Jill is preparing for the perfect night of sleep. She had no coffee after 10 am. She drank a warm cup of milk with honey after dinner. She had a soothing bath filled with Epsom salts. She hung blackout curtains in her bedroom and she set the temperature to eighteen degrees Celsius, which she had read was optimal for sleep.

---

33 Zaccaro, A., Piarulli, A., Laurino, M., Garbella, E., Menicucci, D., Neri, B., & Gemignani, A. (2018). How breath-control can change your life: a systematic review on psycho-physiological correlates of slow breathing. *Frontiers in human neuroscience*, 353.

"Nothing is going to prevent me from getting a great sleep tonight," she tells herself.

Unfortunately, a newly married couple just moved in next door.

Not even Jill's noise-blocking headphones could quiet the sound of the headboard jarring against her wall. She knew this year's neighborhood block party would be an awkward one.

At least her slow breathing allows her to manage her irritation better!

A PERSONALIZED BREATHING PRESCRIPTION

STEVEN, A CAR MECHANIC, is meeting with his doctor because he has been feeling dizzy and lightheaded in recent weeks—not to mention more irritable and quicker to fly off the handle with customers.

His doctor takes Steven's blood pressure. It is too high.

Our blood pressure is an automatic function. It is happening without our conscious direction. But we can influence our blood pressure through our breath. For instance, snoring loudly and stopping the breath during sleep increase blood pressure, while breathing hard and fast and feeling stressed also elevate blood pressure.

Steven is indeed stressed at work, and it is easily apparent to the doctor that his breathing is hard and fast. So, he performs an assessment.

The number of breaths per minute during normal breathing is about 12 to 14. Each breath is approximately 500 ml of air. This provides a healthy volume of 5 to 6 liters of air per minute. Steven's breathing pattern amounts to 12 liters of air per minute.

"You are breathing too much air," the doctor states. "Just like putting too much air into a tire is not advisable, neither is over-breathing. It results in a reduction of blood flow and oxygen delivery to the brain, and a tire unsafe for any use outside of CrossFit."

"So, how should I breathe?" demands Steven, still irritable.

"You are at rest and you are breathing 20 or more breaths per minute. I want you to slow down your breathing and avoid taking big breaths in and out."

"Slow down my breathing," repeats Steven, incredulously.

"Yes. Ideally, everyone would take only 12 to 14 breaths per minute. But it's important to slow down your breathing relative to your current breathing rate. If I instructed you to slow down your breathing to 6 breaths per minute, taking 4 seconds to breathe in and 6 seconds to breathe out, you would feel uncomfortable, and it could even make your symptoms worse. Since you are breathing on average 20 breaths per minute during rest, it is too much to try to slow down your breathing to 6 breaths per minute. However, I think 12 breaths per minute is realistic."

Steven is instructed to breathe in softly and silently through his nose for a count of 2 seconds and out softly and silently for a count of 3 seconds. After just a few minutes of this breathing pattern, Steven remarks that he feels somewhat better.

It's important to remember that breathing is not "one size fits all." Just as Steven's doctor advised him to slow his breathing relative to his *own* current breathing rate, it's important that you slow your breathing relative to *your own* rate. But you don't need to see a doctor to find out what will work best for you.

Simply take your BOLT score and use it to guide your breathing practice, initially performing each exercise for no more than 2 minutes. Take a gentle approach to doing the exercises and build up your breathing practice gradually. Over time, you will see improvements in your BOLT score and you can use this to monitor your progress.

Like Steven, if your everyday breathing is, say, 14 breaths per minute, then you could practice slowing down your breathing. Aim for a point where you breathe in for 3 seconds and out softly and silently for 5 seconds, all through the nose. Or you could take it one step further and breathe in softly for 4 seconds and out softly for 6 seconds.

Slowing down the breathing or respiratory rate helps to bring body and mind into balance. It reduces the stress response and activates the relaxation response, and therefore, will result in a healthier, more stable blood pressure.

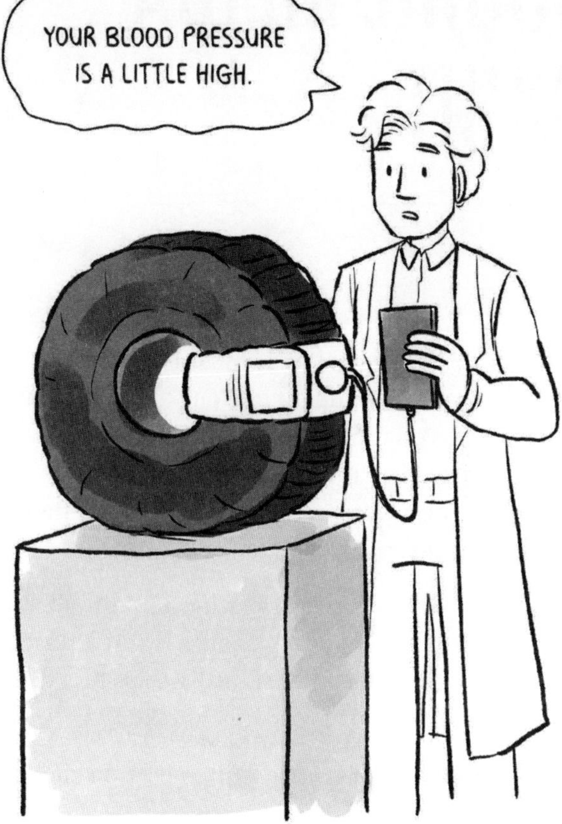
YOUR BLOOD PRESSURE IS A LITTLE HIGH.

A BREATH-TAKING SOCIAL MEDIA HABIT

YOUR BREATHING IS CLOSELY CONNECTED to your mental, emotional, and physical well-being. Holding your breath too often and for too long can cause your stress and anxiety levels to increase. This is the case with Roger, who has developed a habit of both faster breathing and breath-holding when scrolling social media, though he doesn't know it yet.

At every opportunity, Roger reaches into his pocket and takes out his phone to scroll through TikTok, Instagram, and Facebook. Scrolling social media helps him deal with boredom, or at least that's what he thinks.

Roger simply cannot just sit still and be in the present moment.

He constantly scrolls through photos of beautiful people who always appear happy, on holiday, or eating a mouthwatering meal. The majority of young men seem to have shaven, chiseled chests and six-pack abs, while the young women have luscious hair and their make-up is perfect. Everyone looks perfect, their lives even more so.

"I wonder if I could be an influencer," Roger asks himself, glancing down at his hairy belly and plate of cold pasta perched on top of it. This constant comparison agitates Roger, and yet, he still scrolls.

As Roger compares his life and apparent shortcomings with those of others on social media, he unintentionally holds his breath.

Most nights, Roger's sleep quality suffers as a consequence of his habit. When he should be winding down for the night, his mind is over-stimulated as he swipes through online posts. The content provokes a range of emotions—surprise, suspense, sadness, joy, jealousy, excitement, and anticipation. As his emotions stir while he processes this content, his body's natural response is to breathe faster and, at times, briefly hold its breath.

Roger's mind never finds complete rest. Any downtime is filled by wading through the constant stream of personal updates and alluring online content.

Roger is not alone. It is not uncommon for people to spend an excessive amount of time scrolling social media on a daily basis, and it's important to become aware of how our breathing can be affected while consuming social media.

We can regain control and develop healthier scrolling habits by consciously slowing down our breathing and breathing through our noses together with avoiding holding our breath for long durations after inhalations.

Mark Zuckerburg, the CEO of Facebook, is worth $165 billion, solely because people like Roger give him two to three hours of personal time every day for free. Imagine willingly giving two to three hours of your time every day to scrolling on social media—making one individual very wealthy and ruining your mental health in the process.

What could you achieve with two to three hours of daily commitment to a positive goal? Or even just a few minutes focusing on improving your breathing techniques every day?

SOAKED AND STRESSED: A BREATHLESS JOB QUEST

THE DAY OF JACOB'S LONG-AWAITED interview has arrived. He had applied four times in the last two years for a position at the largest technology company in his hometown.

During that time, he completed a number of computer science courses and therefore felt he was now a more suitable candidate. Now, he sits, fidgeting, in the waiting room, preparing for the interview.

Just before the interview starts, he goes to the bathroom. Unfortunately, while washing his hands, he manages to soak the front of his trousers and there's no time to dry them. This wouldn't have been too bad if he had worn his dark suit pants. But no. Today, he had to have on his light-colored slacks—the ones he'd purchased just for the occasion—and the wet patch was clearly visible to anyone within fifty yards. He's now stressed, and suddenly, his breathing becomes faster and harder.

Not only is he nervous, but now he also feels embarrassed as he takes a slightly sodden seat in front of the interview panel.

During the interview, the more he tells himself to calm down, the faster and harder his breathing becomes.

Your brain interprets this type of breathing as a sign that your body is under threat. The mind is not able to tell the difference between an imagined threat and a real threat. As long as your breathing is a little harder and faster, that's a trigger for the brain to launch the body into survival mode, increasing your heart rate and urging you to get away from the situation. But during an interview is not the time to get up out of your chair, no matter how stressed you might be.

The interview panel thanks Jacob for coming and tells him they will be in contact soon.

"Great. Another rejection note for the file," Jacob thinks to himself sourly.

Jacob is right.

Two weeks later, a rejection letter arrives in the mail. It states that there were more qualified applicants, but Jacob strongly believed the real reason he was not hired was because the interview panel could sense his discomfort and then assumed that he wouldn't be up for the task. Well, that, and his soaked trousers. Don't let your breathing let you down.

CV

THREE YEARS IN ECONOMICS SCHOOL

TWO YEARS IN FINANCE

TEN YEARS IN NERVOUS

FOUR YEARS IN ANXIETY

ELEVEN YEARS IN STRESSED

NAMA-STAY QUIET

EMMA IS SUFFERING FROM ANXIETY. She has a stressful job and two hyperactive kids.

She joins a yoga class to help her relax.

The instructor tells the class to take silent and slow breaths in and out through the nose. Throughout the asanas, breathing could not be heard from anyone in the class.

"By the late 19th century, 70–90% of the urban populations of Europe and North America were infected with tuberculosis. There was a belief at the time that germs would spread more easily if lungs were not fully ventilated. The idea was that "He lives most life whoever breathes most air."[34] Deep breathing started to thrive and spread all over Europe, America, and India by the 1880s. It's amazing the impact, for better or worse, that one idea can have when properly executed.

But originally, yoga breathing meant subtle, quiet breaths in through the nose and slow, really relaxed breaths out through the nose. "That's how we practice here," the instructor explains as the class packs up.

---

34 Evans. W. F. (1886). *Esoteric Christianity and mental therapeutics*. HH Carter & Karrick.

"I thought bigger was better," remarks one student.

"It's all about how you use it!" responds the instructor with a cheeky wink.

All the attendees laugh.

"Laughter is good," continues the instructor. "Laughing is wonderful for releasing tension. Also, as strange as it may sound, as you are breathing, scan your body for areas of tension and practice consciously relaxing that area as well as your entire body from head to toe. Allow positive energy and thoughts to enter your body as you inhale and release negative energy as you exhale."

BREATHING ON-TARGET

JEREMY IS LEARNING ARCHERY.

"Why can't I ever hit the center of the target?" he complains to his coach.

"Maybe you'd have better luck aiming for the department store building," jokes the coach.

"Very funny" Jeremy replies, rolling his eyes.

"The reason you keep missing is because you are too tense. Forget the target. Close your eyes. Now, breathe quietly in through your nose for 4 seconds. Then exhale quietly and gently through your nose for 6 seconds. Do that 5 times" instructs the coach. Jeremy does as he's told, leveling his bow.

"Now, look at the target and prepare to aim. After you breathe in gently with your nose, exhale quietly and gently, and just towards the bottom of the breath—shoot the arrow. Breathe into the shot. . . ."

Jeremy releases the arrow.

"Bullseye!" exclaims the instructor. "Well done."

A NOSE FOR RECOVERY

EVER SINCE HE WAS A TODDLER, John seemed almost indefatigable. He had enormous strength and determination. Neither lack of sleep nor stress seemed to bother him. He excelled both academically and athletically.

However, during his senior year of high school, an accidental elbow to his face during a football game resulted in a broken nose.

A nose breather all his life, John now has to resort to breathing through his mouth.

Forced to slow down and rest in bed, it seems like John's injury together with his fast-paced, ambitious lifestyle has caught up with him.

When his doctor comes to visit him, he diagnoses John as having chronic fatigue. The doctor explains to John in football terms that he is like a quarterback trying to throw a long, touchdown pass but his hands are tied together.

To make matters worse, mouth breathing is causing John to breathe in a slightly faster and harder manner than normal which was sending a signal to his brain that things are not okay.

Three weeks later, John's nose has healed and his condition and sense of well-being are fast improving.

John resumes taking soft breaths in and relaxed, slow breaths out through his nose. The healing and recovery process could now fully commence since this pattern of breathing is telling his brain that the body is safe. The brain responds by sending signals of calm to the body.

TAKE A DEEP BREATH

WITH FINAL EXAMS FAST APPROACHING, Jolie is feeling overwhelmed and her mind is full of negative thoughts.

Noticing how preoccupied her daughter's mind has become, Jolie's mom purposely let out a scream, causing Jolie to dash upstairs to check on her mom.

Although she was upset that her mom made her worry for nothing, in that moment she was not thinking about her exams. She's relieved and, as a result, her breathing slows down which also has a calming effect on her body and mind.

"I cleared your mind," her mom tells her proudly. "Now, please go downstairs and clear the dirty dishes off the table."

Jolie, trudging back down the stairs, considers the whole thing a terrible charade.

Jolie might let out a long sigh as she takes care of her household chores, but what she doesn't know is that breathing deeply actually has its own benefits. But how exactly can you access them?

We're going to get into it in the next chapter!

A summary of all the breathing exercises and some recommendations for breathing to calm body and mind and improve sleep quality is included at the end of the book.

BREATHE DEEP

WHILE WAITING IN LINE FOR the women's toilet, Monica is practicing proper breathing.

She knows that to breathe properly, you must keep your chest still and breathe through your nose.

Nose breathing results in breathing low into the diaphragm, while mouth breathing results in breathing into the upper chest.

Monica has one hand on her chest and one just above her belly button. As she inhales through her nose, her belly gently moves out. As she exhales through her nose, her belly gently moves in.

The lady at the front of the line turns around and sees Monica's hand on her belly.

"You must've had the spicy curry," she tells her sympathetically. "I ran out the back door in the middle of a date the last time I made that mistake in here! Go ahead of me, I insist."

A CHEEKY LESSON ON BREATHING

CONOR IS ATTENDING A WRESTLING CAMP in Russia to hone his skills.

During the warm-up, the coach, Pavel, who speaks with a thick Russian accent, curtly orders students to "Breathe through your backsides."

Confused, Conor replies, "backsides?"

"Ves, ves," the coach responded, which Conor took to mean yes.

Still confused, Conor was wondering if the coach truly wanted him to try to breathe out his backside, that is, his bum. So, after getting the coach's attention, Conor pointed at his bum.

"No," responds the coach, rolling his eyes, before touching Conor's back as well as his ribs at the sides of his body.

"Aha," Conor realizes. "You want me to breathe with optimal movement of the diaphragm which causes my back and ribs to gently move outwards?"

"Ves, ves," the coach confirms.

This type of diaphragmatic breathing is often called "belly breathing." An issue with this terminology is that people can push and pull their bellies out and in without even breathing.

True diaphragmatic breathing involves silently breathing through the nose when at rest. With diaphragmatic breathing, your mid-to-lower back and the sides of your body will move outwards with each inhalation and inwards with each exhalation. And that is what the coach meant by breathing through their backsides. He wants the students' backs and the sides of their bodies to move out and in with each breath.

"That's what I get for ass-uming," Conor sheepishly replies while practicing diaphragmatic breathing.

BACK TO BREATHING BASICS

ROY IS VISITING HIS DOCTOR due to neck and lower back pain.

He's a truck driver and assumes that his neck and lower back pain are the result of sitting for long periods at a time, together with the fact that he has gained some weight in recent years.

At the medical clinic, his doctor agrees that his neck and lower back pain may in part be explained by his sedentary job and weight gain.

However, when listening to Roy's lungs using his stethoscope, the doctor notices that Roy breathes through his mouth and into his upper chest.

The doctor informs Roy that it is not uncommon for people with chronic low back pain to breathe differently compared to people free from low back pain.

"There is a muscle located towards the bottom of your rib cage called the diaphragm. It should be doing most of the work when you breathe. However, in your case and for many others with neck and low back pain, the diaphragm is being underutilized."

The doctor continued, "You are breathing with muscles in your chest. When you breathe using these muscles, you are causing stress, strain, and compression through your spine. Using your diaphragm to breathe will result in decreased neck and lower back pain—especially in combination with losing some weight and including more standing and movement throughout your workday."

"How do I breathe with my diaphragm?" asks Roy.

"Firstly, I want you to close your mouth and place your tongue on the roof of your mouth behind your front teeth. With your mouth closed you will have to breathe through your nose. Breathing through the nose increases the use of the diaphragm. Conversely, breathing through the mouth decreases recruitment of the diaphragm. Next, place your hands on your lower ribs. As you breathe in, gently guide your ribs outward. As you breathe out, gently guide your ribs inward."

The doctor plants his hands either side of his body to demonstrate.

"Put your hands on either side of your body to feel the movement of your lower ribs. Place your attention on your breath. As you breathe in, gently guide your lower ribs to move outward. As you breathe out, gently encourage your lower ribs to move inward. Continue to breathe in this way. As you breathe in, the lower ribs move outward and

as you breathe out, the lower ribs move inward. Excellent job. Well done."

"That's great. You used your diaphragm. Now, when exhaling, your lower ribs move inwards. Well done, Roy!"

If you are new to diaphragmatic breathing, begin by practicing for 2 or 3 minutes, 3 times a day—you can do it whenever you have some free time, such as standing in line for the bank, waiting for a file to download, or standing at the school gates to pick up your kids. There's always an opportunity to improve your breathing! Gradually increase how long and how often you do diaphragmatic breathing. Over time, you will do it naturally. Breathing in this way should help reduce any stress, tension, and strain in your neck and back.

"Thanks, doctor," remarks Roy. "If I start breathing with my diaphragm, is it still necessary for me to lose weight?"

"Let's get an X-ray for that funny bone next time you come in. It may be faulty," the doctor teases him.

"TECH-NECK"
AND BREATH

DR. JORDAN, A SPINE SURGEON, is giving a presentation at a conference on the relationship between posture and health.

"Long hours spent looking down at a book or electronic devices—from mobile phones to computers, laptops, and tablets—can put undue pressure on your neck, spine, and shoulders."

"This can lead to a number of ailments, including headaches, stiff necks, herniated discs, and even permanent abnormal curvature of the spine, leading to a hunch-backed appearance, or what is now commonly called "tech-neck". And with data showing that people are spending more and more hours per day on electronic devices, the number of patients reporting "tech-neck" related issues is likely to get worse," he lectures to his enthralled audience.

The spine surgeon shows a slide with a photo of someone with a "tech-neck," which had the unintentional effect of causing members of the audience to look around and assess one another's posture while straightening up themselves.

"Another lesser-known problem connected with looking down at either digital devices or a book for long periods of time is impaired breathing," continues the spine surgeon. "When your spine is rounded forward, it makes it difficult to breathe, because your shoulders and rib cage are limiting the expansion of your lungs. This type of shallow breathing leads to a lack of oxygen supply to the brain which can result in ailments such as lightheadedness, foggy thinking, and tension headaches."

The spine surgeon finishes his presentation with some tips to prevent "tech-neck" and impaired breathing while using digital devices and reading—including raising books and electronic devices to eye level and standing and sitting with proper neck alignment and posture.

Lastly, he says to his audience "I look forward to us playing many more rounds of golf together. But if some of you don't correct your posture and breathing, the only back nine you'll be doing is nine appointments on my table!"

Though this particular lecture is totally strait-laced, there are plenty of benefits to engaging with LSD when it comes to breathing—don't believe me? Let me convince you!

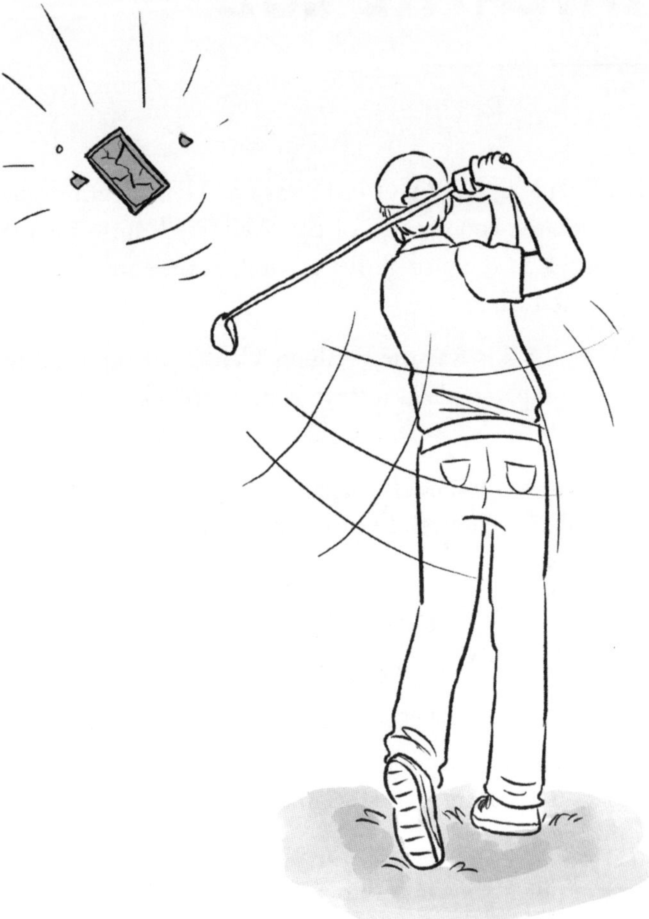

BREATHE LSD

JUST AS THE PARTICIPANTS ARE greeting one another, the coordinator of the Wellness Centre for the Elderly asks them to gather around, as they are about to try some LSD.

"I thought this was the Wellness Centre for the Elderly, not some psychedelic retreat!" one participant pipes up, outraged.

"I'm sorry, ma'am. I didn't mean that kind of LSD. Here at our wellness center, LSD is an abbreviation for our breathing approach."

"Thank goodness," exhales the participant, relieved.

"Let me explain," announces the coordinator.

"The letter 'L' stands for **Light** (breathing). We want you to soften and reduce the volume of air that you breathe to achieve a comfortable sensation of breathlessness."

"The letter 'S' stands for **Slow** (breathing). We want you to slow down your respiratory rate so that you are taking fewer breaths per minute."

"The letter 'D' stands for **Deep** (breathing). We want you to breathe into the lower region of the lungs."

"That's it—LSD. You will practice breathing lightly, slowly, and deeply. Better health and well-being will be the by-product."

One of the female participants turns to another female participant and remarks, "I haven't had a cigarette in 30 years. I haven't had a drop of alcohol in 20 years. I'm not allowed to consume sugar or bacon, and I can't remember the last time I had sex. I don't know about you, but I think I would have been open to trying some LSD!"

BALANCE

IT'S SATURDAY MORNING, which, for Paul, means reading military-related magazines.

Paul is obsessed with all things military.

That morning, when he declined a friend's invite to play basketball, his friend said he was boring and called him "a square."

"How did you know I practice box breathing?" Paul asks, surprised.

"What's your angle here?" his friend shoots back.

Soldiers know that if they are stressed, they are likely to make mistakes. Therefore, as part of their training, soldiers are exposed to various stressors to help them adapt to stress.

Soldiers also practice a breathing technique called "box breathing," known in the military as "tactical breathing."

Tactical breathing involves breathing in through the nose silently and softly for a count of 4 seconds, then holding the breath for a count of 4 seconds before exhaling through the nose silently and softly for a count of 4 seconds and finally holding for a count of 4 seconds.

So, box breathing consists of 4 sequences that are equal in length just like a box consists of 4 equal sides—hence the name.

If breathing tactics work for highly trained special operations personnel, then they can work for us, too.

DON'T HOLD YOUR BREATH!

BARBARA IS TWO WEEKS INTO a 30-day health challenge, which includes doing box breathing and breath holds through her nose, 3 times a day.

In her professional life, Barbara is a successful business strategist who is particularly skilled at identifying where a company is allocating 80% of its resources yet only generating 20% of its output and vice versa.

Unfortunately, she doesn't apply the same skillset when it comes to breathing.

While her 30-day challenge is going well, apart from the times she does box breathing and breath holds, her breathing is poor.

Barbara tends to breathe with her mouth. She also breathes loudly and far too fast. During times of stress, she also has a habit of holding her breath, sometimes to the point where she is turning blue in the face.

In other words, Barbara is breathing incorrectly far more than 80% of the time. If she were to analyze her breathing patterns, she would know she was in the red, with very little return on investment.

Box breathing and other breathing techniques, like breath holding, provide numerous benefits. But ultimately, breathing well is not about what you do occasionally, but consistently.

When you walk, dance, practice yoga, or engage in any form of movement, effective breathing should be incorporated into your practice. This means breathing in and out through your nose and breathing lightly and slowly.

Similarly, before sleep, soften your breathing with a gentle inhale and slow relaxed exhale. Doing so sends a signal to your brain that your body is safe, promoting better sleep quality.

And speaking of sleep—how you breathe has a huge impact on how you sleep. Let's explore how certain breathing techniques can impact sleep, both positively and negatively—and how a trip to *Vagus* can help!

SLEEP

RONAN HAS HAD TWO WEEKS of terrible sleep. He is struggling with falling asleep.

The list of sleep aids he has tried is a long one—melatonin supplements, chamomile tea, lavender drops on his pillow, blackout curtains, white noise, hypnosis, no caffeine after noon, no alcohol, hot baths, cold showers, a weighted blanket, a special acupressure pillow, and ear plugs . . . he should try counting those instead of sheep to help him sleep!

His friend and colleague, Joe, who is concerned that Ronan's health and well-being are suffering due to his sleep deprivation, suggests looking into the vagus nerve.

Ronan loves Las Vegas, and he recently heard that U2 is now a resident band at The Sphere, so he would love to go visit—but doesn't understand how doing so would improve his sleep . . . plus he's far too busy to take time off from work to make the trip.

"No," interrupts Joe. "Not Las Vegas! I'm talking about the vagus nerve. The "vagus" that leaves you waking up *without* regret."

Taking light, slow, quiet, deep breaths in and out through the nose is a great way to stimulate the vagus nerve.

To prime your body for a better night's rest, breathe lightly, taking in less air for 5 to 10 minutes before attempting to fall asleep. Using your nose, breathe about 30% less air into your body. When exhaling, do so in a gentle, quiet, and relaxed manner. You will feel a sensation of breathlessness, but it should be tolerable. Continue to breathe softly; so softly that you feel hardly any air entering your nose. Imagine there is a feather under your nostrils, and you do not want to make it move as you breathe.

"There are two things you should never gamble on: video poker and your sleep," jokes Joe.

THE SLEEP SOLUTION

TARA IS PREPARING TO SIT an important exam. She has studied hard but still feels a little uneasy. That night she falls asleep, only to find herself lying awake in bed at 3 am.

She also woke up at about 3am on Saturday morning, but since Saturday was her day off and she had no exam—she didn't care and fell back asleep after a short while.

But this morning is different as she has an exam to complete in a few hours' time. She finds herself in limbo—not alert enough to get up, nor tired enough to fall back asleep.

She also knows that if she doesn't fall back asleep, she will be exhausted when it is time to get up. Now the pressure is on, and, as she lies there, her mind races from one thought to another.

It's an unfortunate truth that trying to fall asleep hampers falling asleep. Instead, hand the problem over to something else.

Whenever I am due to give a presentation and wake up in the middle of the night before my talk, my go-to strategy is to listen to myself speaking a 20-minute guided audio for insomnia. My phone is in flight mode, I put on headphones, hit play, and relax. As I listen to the instructions, my thoughts begin to settle, I feel sleepy, and I fall asleep.

Remember—the next time you wake up in the middle of the night, you have a much better chance of falling back asleep by handing the problem over to something else. Listen to my guided audio or any guided audio that has been specially written for getting back to sleep quickly.

The audio is available free on Spotify or YouTube. Simply search for "Patrick McKeown guided audio insomnia."

SNORE NO MORE

DIANA HAS BEEN EXHAUSTED SINCE moving in with her boyfriend Frank, who snores.

Breathing through your mouth at night makes you more likely to snore and wake up with a dry mouth.

Diana asks Frank to sleep in the basement next to the dog, but every time he snores, the dog barks. Frustrated, Diana asks her friend Leslie for advice.

"Try this," Leslie said, reaching into her bag and pulling out a strip of cotton elasticated tape kind of shaped like an O called *MyoTape*.

"Why do you have this?" Diana asks, wrinkling her nose in confusion. "Does Peter snore?"

"Not anymore," she replies with a wink, pointing at My O Tape.

Prior to using MyoTape (which he uses to gently bring his lips together so that he breathes through his nose during the night), her husband, Peter, had been snoring through his mouth. He would also wake up several times throughout the night and would have to drink water to soothe his dry mouth and throat—symptoms of mouth breathing.

The air we breathe contains moisture from our respiratory tract as we exhale. Unlike the mouth, the nose contains a tissue called the nasal mucosa that helps to capture and recycle this moisture, reducing water loss from the body.

Mouth-taping during sleep has been found to improve snoring and the severity of sleep apnea in mouth-breathers by up to 50%.[35] I particularly recommend MyoTape, as it is placed around the lips (rather than across the mouth) and is designed to act as a reminder, using elastic tension to encourage the lips together yet still permitting the person to open their mouth should they wish to.

35   E.G. Lee, Y. C., Lu, C. T., Cheng, W. N., & Li, H. Y. (2022). The Impact of Mouth-Taping in Mouth-Breathers with Mild Obstructive Sleep Apnea: A Preliminary Study. Healthcare (Basel, Switzerland), 10(9), 1755.

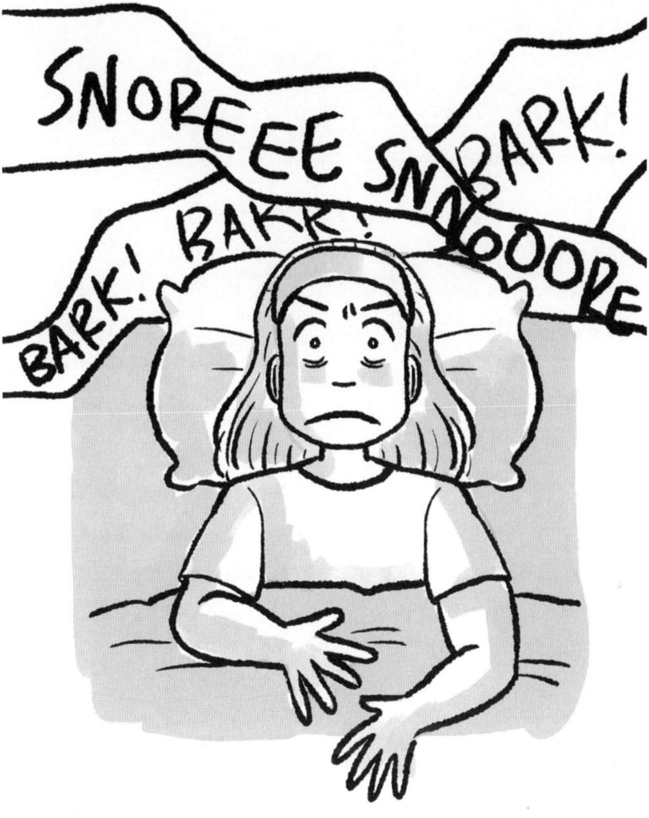
SNOREEE SNNOOORE
BARK!
BARK! BARK!

SILENT NIGHT

THE MAIN CAUSES OF SNORING are obstructed airways and heavier breathing.

Breathing involves air moving through the respiratory system—which includes the nose, mouth, throat, voice box, windpipe, and lungs. When airflow through the nose and throat is partially blocked, it causes resistance to breathing. When the resistance is high enough, it causes snoring and worst of all may involve stopping of the breath called "sleep apnea."

Various factors can cause airways to be partially blocked, including underdevelopment of the face (remember Harvold's famous study on monkeys), allergies or colds, a deviated septum, enlarged tonsils, or being overweight and obese.

Although air can enter the respiratory system through the nose or the mouth, breathing through the mouth results in increased blockage of the airways.

Try it for yourself: first, open your mouth and make the sound of a snore through it. Now, try to snore through your mouth with your mouth closed. You will find it impossible to snore when your mouth is closed.

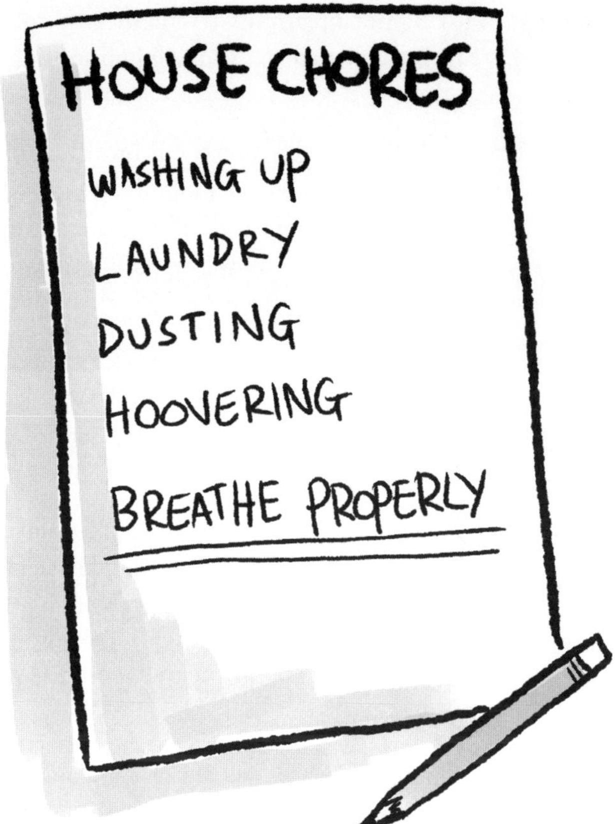
HOUSE CHORES
WASHING UP
LAUNDRY
DUSTING
HOOVERING
BREATHE PROPERLY

Next, make the sound of a snore through your nose. Trying to snore through your nose sounds different than mouth snoring. To observe the connection between your breathing patterns and snoring, gently soften and slow down your breathing. With lighter breathing, try to snore through your nose. While possible to do so, you will find snoring to be much reduced.

How we breathe during the day affects our breathing patterns throughout the night. Having a higher BOLT score implies that breathing is lighter both during the day and during sleep. With lighter and slower breathing, snoring and sleep apnea reduce during sleep.

Furthermore, you can help open your airways to improve airflow and reduce the chances of snoring. Simply keep your lips together and rest your tongue on the roof of the mouth.

Another useful tactic is to breathe light and slow during the day. Practice breathing less air during the day so that you feel a tolerable need for air. Begin with practicing for just a few minutes, and build up from there. Ten minutes is good. Two ten-minute sessions during the day are better. Three ten-minute sessions are excellent.

If you have a roommate or share a bed with someone, they will certainly be thankful.

ASTHMA

ASTHMA IS A CONDITION IN which the passages of the windpipe and lungs narrow and swell, triggering feelings of chest tightness, wheezing, and coughing.

Whitney has suffered from asthma for many years. Her classmates used to tease and call her wheezing Whitney, but to her and her family, asthma was no laughing matter.

Luckily for Whitney, her life is about to change thanks to a passenger riding the same train as her on an otherwise unassuming Monday morning.

Running late, like she always does, Whitney sprints to make it to the train—triggering, as it so often did, a mild asthma attack. When she takes her seat, she reaches into her bag and pulls out an inhaler.

While most seniors in high school made sure not to leave home without their smartphones, in Whitney's case, her top priority is to never leave home without her inhaler. She takes a few puffs, settling her lungs as best she can, and vows to start setting her alarm to awaken her earlier, to avoid getting caught out like this. She's a high school student, not an Olympic sprinter, and doing one-hundred-meter dashes up the platform every morning is not good for her.

Noticing Whitney's distress, an older lady, a retired nurse, takes a seat next to Whitney and takes Whitney's mind off her troubles by sharing details about her day.

After developing some rapport, the lady, nearing her nineties, shares with Whitney that her husband once suffered from asthma.

"When his asthma got so bad that his inhaler was getting more action in the bedroom than I was, I knew I had to find a solution," she laughs, shaking her head. Whitney's cheeks flush. What is she meant to do with this information about this lady's bedroom activities? The nurse continues quickly, noticing the teenager's confusion.

"My husband was a mouth breather. I watched you as you got on the train, and I believe you are too".

"Is that bad?" asks Whitney.

"A good doctor told my husband that mouth breathing makes asthma worse. Breathing through an open mouth not only leaves your airways unprotected from cold, dry air, and airborne viruses, bacteria, allergens, and other particles, but it can easily result in breathing too much air, which can inflict trauma on the airways, causing swelling, inflammation, and airway narrowing."

"If the airways cool or become too dry, they narrow, and this makes breathing difficult. Learning to breathe through the nose is logical as the nose warms and moistens the incoming air, and produces its own supply of the gas nitric oxide, which helps keep the airways open."

Whitney tries to take it all in, wondering if she can whip out her notebook and scribble some of this down.

"My husband had asthma for a number of decades and the solution was simply to breathe through his nose and to practice breathing less air. When you take less air into the lungs for short periods of time during the day, the airways open, making breathing easier. Try it. Take a soft breath into your nose and allow a slow and relaxed breath out. Soften your breathing so that you are breathing less air than you normally would. The goal is to create a sensation that you need more air. Doing this for 3 to 4 minutes a number of times throughout the day helps to open the airways," she finishes up, with a kind smile. "It worked wonders for my husband!"

"No way?!" Whitney replies, flabbergasted.

"Yes, way," she chuckles, shaking her head.

"In just three months, my husband's use of rescue medication decreased by 90% and preventative medication decreased by half. He rarely coughed or wheezed at all, and the only time he experienced tightness in the chest or breathlessness was when I wore the red dress that he loved so much," she continues, giggling like a schoolgirl.

Whitney can't help herself—she busts out with laughter, before telling the lady that she'd love to meet her husband. The woman's face softens slightly, a sadness tinging her eyes.

"Unfortunately, Roger is no longer with us. He passed away from natural causes one year ago, but he would have liked you."

Whitney touches her hand lightly, doing her best to comfort her.

"If you don't mind me asking, how did you two meet?" asks Whitney.

"He was a carpenter. One day, he cut his hand and went to the hospital for stitches. I was the one who cleaned his wound. I couldn't refuse when he asked me to go for ice cream that evening. He was so charming and witty. By the end of the night, he had me in stitches as well."

Soon after their encounter on the train, Whitney attends her local hospital to examine her breathing volume. The test showed that her breathing volume was 15 liters per minute, far higher than a normal breathing volume of 4 to 6 liters per minute.

Whitney told her doctor that she was going to breathe only through her nose and to stop over-breathing. But the doctor just stood there as if Whitney had two heads.

At first, it seemed strange to Whitney that she might be breathing too much air. Her problem, after all, is that she felt she was not getting enough air. But the penny eventually dropped—her poor breathing habits were causing her airways to narrow.

With narrow airways, she felt that she was not getting enough air, so she breathed faster and harder, but this caused her airways to narrow even further.

This is the predicament of every child and adult with asthma.

By breathing less air at different times throughout the day her breathing patterns gradually improved. After just a few weeks, her breathing volume decreased to 9 liters per minute. By addressing her mouth breathing and over-breathing habits, her airways opened and her asthma symptoms decreased significantly.

Whitney's results corresponded with results from the first clinical trial of the Buteyko Method for asthma in the Western world. The Buteyko Method is a breathing technique developed by Ukrainian doctor Konstantin Buteyko in the 1950s. It aims to correct dysfunctional breathing patterns and improve overall health by promoting light, nasal breathing, and reducing hyperventilation (which involves breathing in excess of the body's metabolic needs).

The clinical trial authors reported that participants with asthma who practiced the Buteyko Method techniques had 70% less coughing and wheezing, 90% less need for rescue medication, and 49% less need for inhaled steroid medication—all by learning not to over-breathe.[36]

Whitney's quality of life and ability to stay healthy have increased tremendously. She recently joined a dance class and is considering a career in nursing. And, like any good dancer, she looks so much better performing her moves while breathing in and out through the nose.

---

36 Bowler, S. D., Green, A., & Mitchell, C. A. (1998). Buteyko breathing techniques in asthma: a blinded randomised controlled trial. *Medical journal of Australia, 169*(11-12), 575-578.

But dancing isn't the only sport that can benefit from improved breathing techniques! In the next chapter, we're going to get into how nose breathing can improve running ability—and how cheetahs breathe to support their incredible pace!

RUN, IHOR, RUN

BREATHING THROUGH THE NOSE during physical exercise is bullshit! Yes, that's what I was told recently. The best way to answer that remark is to share a story.

In 1977, James Earl Ray, the assassin of Martin Luther King Jr, escaped from Brushy Mountain State Penitentiary. After running in the woods for nearly fifty-five hours, Ray had covered a distance of only twelve miles. His time was spent hiding from air searches during the day and running around in circles.

Inspired by the jailbreak, Gary Cantrell and Karl Henn founded *Barkley Marathons*. As Ray only covered twelve miles, Gary, a serious ultra runner surmised that he could cover at least a hundred miles.

First run in 1986, the event covers a hundred miles, to be completed in sixty hours across the same terrain that James Earl Ray ran from the authorities. There are no trails, and the only tools that competitors have are a watch, map, and compass. Only twenty-six people have completed the marathon since 1995. The race is so tough that the organizers said a female is unlikely to ever complete it. Well, they were proven wrong in 2024, when Jasmine Paris crossed the line!

In 2024, Ihor Verys completed the marathon with his secret weapon—nasal breathing. Not only did he complete it, but he finished earliest of all the competitors. There is no first, second, or third in this race—there are only finishers. For the naysayers, Ihor Verys' performance is further support for nasal breathing during endurance exercise.

BREATHE SMARTER, NOT HARDER!

RALPH WAS FINDING HIMSELF BECOMING breathless during physical exercise. He followed the same training regimens as his teammates, yet he couldn't keep up with them, leaving his strength and conditioning coach puzzled.

On and off the sports pitch, Ralph is somewhat of a perfectionist in his quest, and he puts high demands on himself. This imposed some stress, which changed his breathing patterns. Ralph's breathing was faster and a little harder than that of his teammates.

Ralph often complains of feeling tired after waking up in the mornings. How he breathed during the day and while exercising influenced how he breathed during sleep.

If your breathing is off during the day, it doesn't automatically correct itself during physical activity or sleep.

Keep in mind that when you first begin practicing nose breathing during physical movement, like any skill, it may be challenging and require a brief period of adaptation.

You will feel that you are not getting enough air. This is because the nose is smaller than the mouth, and the excess carbon dioxide is unable to leave the body so quickly through the nose.

It is the accumulation of carbon dioxide in the blood that influences how breathless you feel during physical exercise. If you continue to breathe through your nose during exercise, your body adapts to tolerate a higher accumulation of carbon dioxide and you will feel less breathless. Your body simply will not need so much air during physical exercise. You have trained yourself to become a more efficient machine.

It's not just about the amount of air that you take into your lungs—what's more important is how much oxygen transfers from the lungs to the blood and from the tissues to working muscles and organs. In fact, with efficient breathing, you don't need as much air to properly oxygenate your body. What is the advantage of this? You don't "gas out" too soon during exercise. You have more reserve in the tank.

Furthermore, the nose can dilate or open wider during exercise to allow for increased airflow (and, as a quick test of your attention—what are the two ways to help decongest the nose?).

This is a natural response to increased demand for oxygen and helps to ensure that the body receives enough oxygen during periods of exertion.

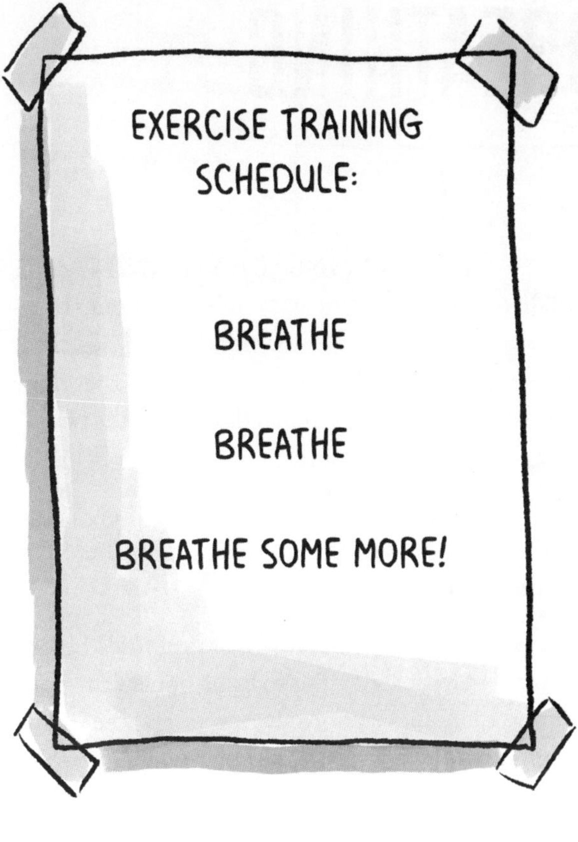
EXERCISE TRAINING
SCHEDULE:
BREATHE
BREATHE
BREATHE SOME MORE!

RECOVERY BREATHING

THE FASTEST-LIVING LAND ANIMAL is the cheetah—it can run up to sixty miles per hour. To ensure sufficient oxygen delivery to the working muscles, the cheetah's respiratory rate can rocket to 150 breaths per minute.[37] In comparison, humans can breathe 50 breaths per minute during high-intensity exercise.

Even if the cheetah manages to catch its prey, it can take 30 minutes for its breathing to calm down before it can enjoy the meal.

If you would rather not wait for 30 minutes before you recover post physical exercise, to bring down your heart and breathing rate quicker, do your best to breathe in and out through the nose in a soft, slow and deep manner. Slowing down your breathing slows down your heart rate. Locate your pulse by feeling your wrist or the carotid artery at the

---

37 https://www.bbcearth.com/news/meet-these-incredible-animal-breathers

angle of your jaw and slow down your breathing to see how soon you can recover after physical exercise.

You might not be able to push your limits as far as the cheetah can, but you are certainly capable of reaching higher levels than you're at now—and breathing can be the groundwork upon which this ability is built.

In the next chapter, let's get into how you can push your limits to take your breathing techniques to the next level!

PUSH YOUR LIMITS

PATRICK IS THE FOUNDER AND DIRECTOR of Education for Oxygen Advantage®, which teaches breathing and focused attention for resilience and improved sports performance. One of the main pillars of the Oxygen Advantage® is to practice holding your breath during movement. This is not suited to people with a BOLT score of less than 15 seconds, people with chronic health conditions (with the exception of mild and moderate asthma), or people over 60 years of age. Breathing is powerful and can have a stronger effect on lowering oxygen and increasing carbon dioxide than the most intense physical exercise.

There are currently more than 5,000 trained Oxygen Advantage® instructors across 50 countries. Just as most personal trainers will tailor a physical exercise program for the client according to age, state of health, and fitness, Oxygen Advantage® breathing instructors also tailor breathing instruction according to age, state of health, and existing breathing patterns.

If you would like to work with one of our breathing instructors, please visit: **OxygenAdvantage.com/instructors** or **Buteykoclinic.com**

BREATH HOLDING FOR THE WIN

WAYNE IS A COLLEGIATE SWIMMER whose performance has improved greatly over the last year despite spending fewer hours in the pool.

So, what has changed?

The only time Wayne breathes through his mouth is when he is swimming, which is fine. Originally, he used to take a breath every three strokes. Now that his body is trained to do more with less, he only needs a breath every five strokes.

When Wayne goes for walks, he breathes in and out through his nose. When running, he also breathes in and out through his nose. If he feels a shortage of air when running more quickly, he will just slow down the pace. During his run, he alters his pace to maintain comfortable nasal breathing.

In addition to this, while running to and from the pool in the mornings, Wayne practices breath holds which he learned from reading *The Oxygen Advantage®* book. Breath-holding is practiced on land, and the goal is to hold the breath until a moderate to strong air hunger is felt.

During his jog, after exhaling through his nose, Wayne gently pinches his nose with his fingers, and with his breath held, he continues to jog until he feels a relatively strong urge to breathe, at which point he lets go of his nose and breathes through it as softly as possible. He then breathes normally for a minute or so while jogging, before repeating this exercise. Typically, on his way to and from the pool, he practices a couple of easy breath holds followed by 3 to 5 stronger breath holds.

Wayne's teammates have recently started calling him "The Shark," which he loves, and joke with him that he must have developed gills. But the truth is he simply changed the way he breathes and incorporates breath holds. He refers to his teammates as dolphins because he can hear them jumping up for air behind him.

Strong breath-holding exercises are only suitable if you are in good health. Consult with your doctor before practicing breath holds if you have any concerns.

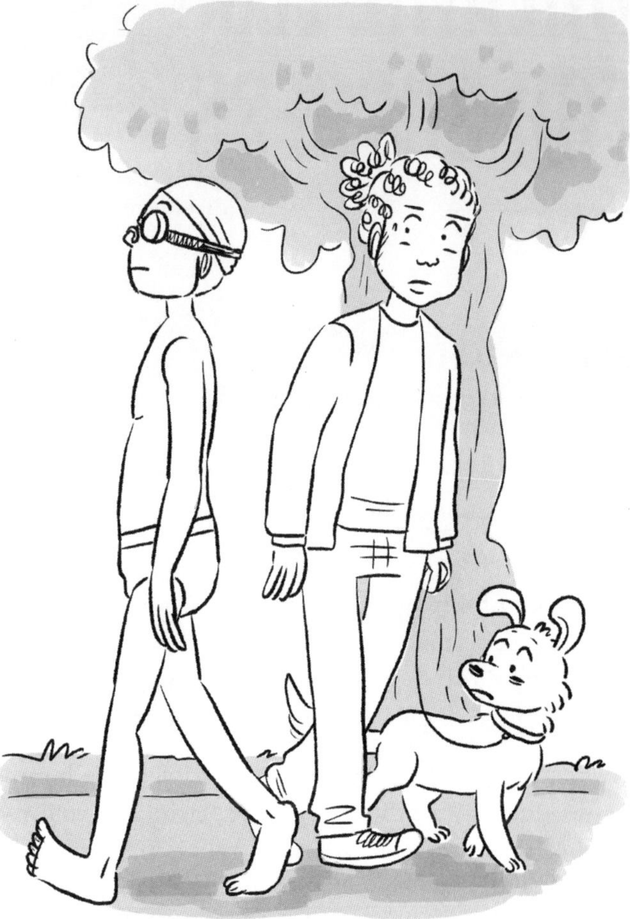

BREATHE LESS FOR SUCCESS

ERIC AND HIS TWIN BROTHER JACOB are delighted—they just received news that their names have both been selected for the Dublin marathon. Eric and Jacob live in different cities but agree to meet once a month for a run to monitor their conditioning.

While running, and during other forms of exercise, your body's need for oxygen increases. At the same time, your body produces more carbon dioxide when physically active. Carbon dioxide causes the hemoglobin in red blood cells to release oxygen to the muscles—this is a good thing.

If you push it hard enough during exercise, as you breathe harder and faster, fatigue begins to set in, and you may have to slow down or even stop. You've hit the wall, as runners say. The demand for oxygen required by your muscles and tissues has exceeded its supply. To delay this happening, you must improve your running economy—that is, your aerobic capacity or your body's ability to use oxygen.

During their first run together, Eric is surprised at how effortlessly his brother Jacob is running. Eric can't keep up and encourages Jacob to run ahead.

Eric is puzzled. While his training routine consists of four runs a week, Jacob is only managing to run twice a week due to his current hectic work schedule.

It isn't all bad news for Eric. His running time is certainly better than the time he set last year for the same distance. Still, he didn't expect his twin brother to outperform him by such a large margin.

"What gives?" pants Eric, after finishing the run.

"Next time, I will carry a few weights to even things up," teases Jacob.

"Seriously, though, what are you doing differently? Are you eating different foods? Are you consuming more energy gels during runs? Is it your shoes? Come on, tell me, bro, what are you doing?" probes Eric.

"Okay, listen. A while back, I read about a study in which scientists reported better running economy in athletes who practice reduced breathing."

He then proceeds to list some of the benefits of breathing light, slow, and deep including improved circulation and oxygen supply to muscles which means you can run faster and longer without getting tired.

Jacob tells his brother that he consciously took fewer breaths per minute, by slowing down the speed at which he inhaled and exhaled. As usual, he breathed in and out through his nose.

"That's it?" replies Eric.

"No, there's more. I also practiced breath holding."

Twice a week during his running sessions, Jacob practiced holding his breath, not after inhalation but after *exhalation*. Every minute for 10 minutes or so, after exhaling the air from his nose, Jacob continued running until he felt a strong urge to inhale. After breathing in, he ran and breathed normally until it was time for the next breath hold. Breath holding during physical exercise causes adaptations to the body, including reduced lactic acid and fatigue.

"Maybe next month, you'll actually be able to keep up with me, and I won't get a crick in my neck from continually looking back to see where you are" jokes Jacob, smirking.

"More like whiplash from me passing you!" Eric laughs.

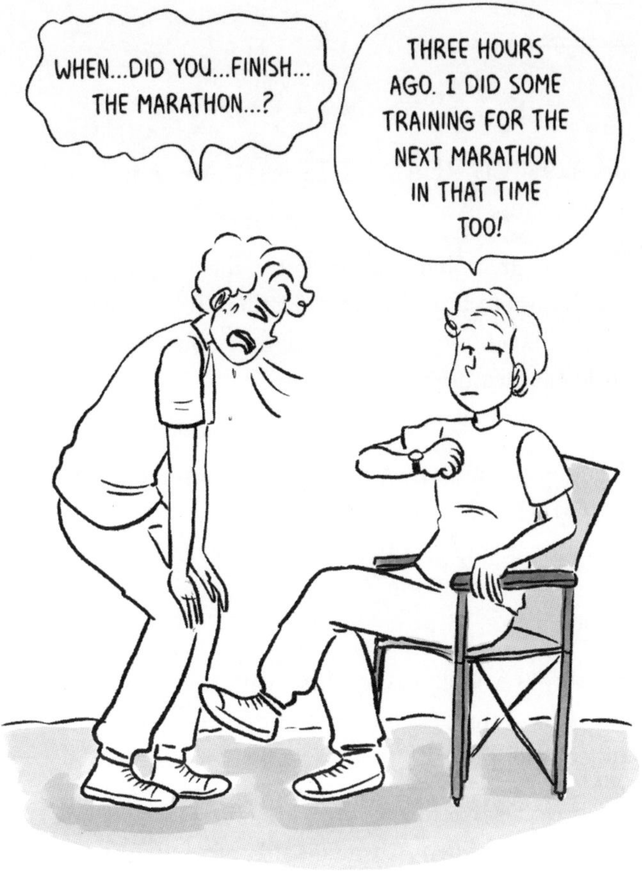
WHEN...DID YOU...FINISH... THE MARATHON...?
THREE HOURS AGO. I DID SOME TRAINING FOR THE NEXT MARATHON IN THAT TIME TOO!

CONCLUSION

SO, YOU'VE READ THIS FAR. Amazing! But have you made use of any of the techniques We've outlined yet?

Theory is great, but practice is the most important thing you can use to improve your breathing techniques. Go try it now—no excuses! Take a break from your day and try out one of the breathing techniques we've covered in this book or check out the exercises on the following pages for guidance.

Whether you're in the midst of situations like the ones we covered with the characters in this book or just trying to create the best grounding for your mind and body to reach their optimal function, you can make use of what you've learned here.

You always have access to your breath, and that means you always have the opportunity to improve your mind, body, and emotional health—no "woo-woo" required!

If you would like to take your breathing journey one step further, the Oxygen Advantage® App is an effective, helpful tool that's also free of charge. We aim to continue to offer the app for free to aid in our goal to generate awareness of the potential of breathing to benefit the physical and mental well-being of everyone.

Oxygen Advantage® is about bringing breathing to the people. There is no guru. There is no tradition. It is an evolving technique based on scientific principles dedicated to generating an awareness of breathing. Our vision is that one day, everyone will know, understand, and apply the power of the breath. The Oxygen Advantage® program exists to empower everyone with optimal breathing as a foundational tool for health, well-being, and performance.

Would You Like to Know More?

If you would like to learn more about the Oxygen Advantage® or the Buteyko Method, take one of our online functional breathing courses, work with one of our certified breathing instructors, or become an instructor yourself. We would love to hear from you!

Check out **OxygenAdvantage.com** if your goal is to improve mental and physical performance.

Check out **ButeykoClinic.com** for specific health complaints such as asthma, anxiety, panic disorder, snoring, and sleep apnea.

Check out **MyoTape.com** for science and application of breathing training to help with insomnia, snoring and obstructive sleep apnea. Here you will also find Kids Corner, where your child can watch videos of Patrick teaching his daughter Lauren how to decongest her nose, better deal with little worries and improve her breathing patterns for sleep, calm and overall health.

SUMMARY OF EXERCISES

I. Breathe Light

The goal of this exercise is to create air hunger to target the biochemical dimension of breathing. (Only suitable for those with a BOLT score greater than 13–14 seconds. If lower, do the **Breathing Recovery Sitting Exercise** instead.)

- Place one hand on your chest and one on your navel.

- Take a soft breath in through your nose and allow a gentle slow relaxed breath out through the nose.

Continue for **3 to 5 minutes. Suitable for all except those with serious medical conditions and those in the first trimester of pregnancy.**

2. Breathe Slow

The goal of this exercise is to help balance the body and mind. During your practice, breathing should be through the nose, slow, and silent.

- Gently breathe in through your nose for 5 seconds.

- Then gently exhale out through your nose for 5 seconds.

Continue for **3 to 5 minutes. Suitable for all persons.**

3. Breathe Deep

The goal of this exercise is to breathe with more optimal movement of the diaphragm.

- Sit or stand with your hands on either side of the lower ribs.

- With your mouth closed, breathe in and out through your nose.

- As you breathe in, you should feel your ribs gently move out, and, as you breathe out, you should feel your ribs gently move in.

- Breathe silently and slowly in for 5 seconds and out for 5 seconds.

Continue for **3 to 5 minutes. Suitable for all persons.**

4. Breathing Recovery Exercise

Anytime you have labored breathing or high stress, do breath holds. This is your emergency breathing exercise:

- Exhale normally through your nose.

- Pinch your nose with your fingers to hold your breath for 5 seconds.

- Let go and breathe normally for 10–15 seconds.

Repeat for **5 to 10 minutes. Suitable for all persons.** If you have anxiety or panic disorder you may use this exercise to decongest your nose, rather than the **Nose Decongesting Exercise** below.

5. Box Breathing

This exercise is about changing states, having balance, and being alert and relaxed at the same time.

- Breathe in for 4 seconds.

- Hold for 4 seconds.

- Breathe out for 4 seconds.

- Hold for 4 seconds.

Repeat for **2 to 4 minutes.** If you find this exercise too challenging, you could start with breathing in for 3 seconds, hold for 3 seconds, breathe out for 3 seconds and hold for 3 seconds.

Suitable for all except those with serious medical conditions and during pregnancy.

6. Nose Unblocking Exercise

- Take a small, light breath in through your nose if you can, and a small breath out through your nose.

- After exhaling, pinch your nose and hold your breath. Keep your lips sealed.

- Gently nod your head or rock your body until you feel that you cannot hold your breath for any longer. You should feel a moderate to strong need for air.

- At this point, let go of your nose, and breathe in gently through it.

- Breathe gently in and out with your mouth closed. When you first breathe in, try to avoid taking a deep breath. Instead, keep your breathing calm and focus on relaxation.

Repeat the exercise **6 times** with a **1-minute rest** between each. **Suitable for those in good health. Not suitable if pregnant, or for those with anxiety or panic disorder.** Those with anxiety or panic disorder could use the **Breathing Recovery Exercise** to decongest their nose.

7. Breath Holding During Movement

This exercise is otherwise known as **Intermittent Hypoxic, Hypercapnic Training (IHHT)**, but that's a bit of a mouthful, so instead, we decided to use the name **"Breath Holding During Movement."** Practicing breath holds whilst walking or jogging helps your breathing become more efficient, opens the airways for easier breathing, and causes positive adaptations to the body, including reduced lactic acid and fatigue.

- Take a normal breath in and out through your nose.

- Pinch and hold your nose.

- Start walking or jogging, whilst holding your breath.

- Continue walking or jogging until you feel a relative air hunger, but don't overdo it.

- Let go and breathe through your nose.

- Continue walking or jogging for about a minute.

Repeat **5 times.** You should be able to recover within 2 to 3 breaths.

> **Long breath holds are not suitable for persons over 60 years of age, during pregnancy, or for anyone with serious health conditions including diabetes, sleep apnea, epilepsy, anxiety, panic disorder, or cardiovascular issues. They are also not suited to people with a BOLT score of less than 15 seconds.**

Pregnancy

For those who are pregnant, we advise the following:

- During your first trimester, practice nose breathing and relaxation only. **Breathe Light** should <u>not</u> be practiced.

- During your second trimester, practice nose breathing, relaxation, and **Breathe Light** with the gentlest of air hunger.

WHAT SHOULD YOU CONCENTRATE ON?

Sleep

To prime your body for a restful night's sleep, practice **Breathe Light,** for **5-10 minutes** before attempting to fall asleep. Using your nose, breathe about 30% less air into your body. When exhaling, do so in a gentle, quiet, and relaxed manner. You will feel a sensation of breathlessness, but it should be tolerable. Continue to breathe softly; so softly that you feel hardly any air entering your nose. Imagine there is a feather under your nostrils, and you do not want to make it move as you breathe. This will help you to fall asleep quickly and wake up feeling alert.

It's very important that you only breathe through your nose while sleeping. This will allow you to wake up feeling refreshed and with a calmer mind. Waking with a dry mouth in the morning is a sign that you are breathing through an open mouth during sleep.

Wearing MyoTape can be a helpful support to safely ensure nasal breathing during sleep. MyoTape is available on **MyoTape.com** (use Promo code Myo10 to receive a 10% discount). Sleeping with your mouth open increases the risk of snoring, insomnia, and obstructive sleep apnea. This can increase the body's stress response—and decrease the relaxation response—which is not at all conducive to enjoying a restorative night's sleep.

If you wake up during the middle of the night and find yourself overthinking—simply play the guided audio for insomnia spoken by Patrick McKeown. This is specially designed to get you "out of your head," induce relaxation, and help you fall back asleep more easily.

At Rest

The best exercise to help improve your BOLT score is **Breathe Light.** Practice this for **4 minutes, 4 to 6 times daily**.

Listen to any of the free guided audios written and spoken by Patrick McKeown once daily.

Guided audios for the topics below are available free of charge from Spotify or YouTube:

- Exam preparation
- Preparation for athletes
- Preparation for musicians
- Insomnia—how to fall back asleep easier
- Perfectionist tendencies

Except for the insomnia recording, a good time to listen to the recordings is straight after lunch to help activate your body's rest and digest response.

Practice the **Breathe Nose, light, Slow, and Deep** exercise for **5 minutes** daily to help activate the diaphragm.

Bring your attention to your breath during your everyday life. By changing your physiology, you will be calmer, more focused, and more productive. Above all else, you will be happier.

Physical Exercise

Always think **Nose, Slow, and Deep** (not Mouth, Fast, and Shallow). Whenever you go for your jog, walk, or run, and no matter what physical movement you are doing, do your best to sustain **Nose, Slow, and Deep**. At first, the air hunger will be stronger because your nose provides a slower entry point than your mouth. That will increase carbon dioxide levels, and, as they increase, you feel the increasing air hunger.

However, if you continue to do your physical exercises with your mouth closed, the air hunger will diminish, and your breathing will become more efficient. Normally, that takes about **5–6 weeks.** At that point, your ventilation, the amount of air you physically need during exercise is reduced, so you will feel less breathless.

If you do physical movement for **30 minutes a day** with your mouth closed, this will improve your breathing patterns. Your degree of breathlessness and your progress can be measured through the **BOLT score.**

You may also practice **Breath Holding During Movement Exercise** (or IHHT) whilst walking or jogging. This not only helps your breathing become more efficient, but it also causes positive adaptations to the body, including increased tolerance of breathlessness during movement, opening the airways for easier breathing, and reduced lactic acid to delay fatigue—so your performance becomes more efficient too.

Stress

Slowing down the breathing or respiratory rate helps to bring body and mind into balance. It reduces the stress response and activates the relaxation response.

When you are feeling stressed, try prolonging your exhalation as this tells your brain that everything is okay. It is the **speed of the exhalation** that determines the body's relaxation response. When you combine air hunger with a longer exhalation, that helps to stimulate the **vagus nerve, promoting a more relaxed state.**

During times of stress, slow down your heart rate and your racing mind with soft, quiet breaths in through the nose followed by gentle, relaxed breaths out through the nose. Practice **Breathe Slow** by breathing in for **3 seconds** and out softly and silently for **5 seconds**, all through the nose. You could take it one step further and breathe in softly for

4 seconds and out softly for **6 seconds**. Continue for **3 to 5 minutes.**

You may also try **humming** as this slows down the speed of the exhalation allowing for more oxygen to be absorbed by the body, as well as stimulating the vagus nerve, helping the body and mind to relax even further. Go to an empty room, sit still and let your body go loose. Take a soft breath in through the nose and hum as you slowly exhale through your nose. Continue for **2 to 5 minutes.**

Concentration

To improve concentration, it's vital to breathe through the nose to promote efficient oxygenation of the cells, tissues, and organs in the body, including the brain. If breathing through your nose is difficult, practice the **Nose Unblocking Exercise,** or **Breathing Recovery Exercise** to decongest your nose.

You may also practice **Breathe Light**, by taking a soft breath in through the nose and allowing a relaxing and slow breath out, to the point of feeling a tolerable air hunger. This will improve your circulation, meaning organs including your brain and heart will receive optimal levels of oxygen, improving concentration and cognitive performance.

ACKNOWLEDGEMENTS

THIS BOOK IS A CULMINATION OF input from many individuals; I am very fortunate to work with such a talented team.

Firstly, a huge thanks to Andrew Dunne for collaborating on this project.

Sincere thanks are due to the Editorial and Design Team: Dr Catherine Bane and Louise McGregor for their valuable insights and for meticulously editing the book's content; Bex Burgess, whose exceptional illustrations breathe life into the text and the book cover design; and Karl Hunt from Karl H Design for typesetting the book.

Thanks also to the outstanding Oxygen Advantage® and Buteyko Clinic International Teams, particularly Jon Murray, Audrey Keogh, and Ana Mahe who do an excellent job at tirelessly running both organizations. Thanks are due also to Tijana Krstović, Ruth Gibney, Orla Kyne, Ronan Maher, and Alessandro Romagnoli.

Thanks to Tom Herron, who I know is always there for us.

Thank you to all the Oxygen Advantage® and Buteyko Clinic Instructors for joining us on the journey.

As ever, special heartfelt thanks to my wife Sinead, and daughter Lauren.

Finally, enormous thanks to you, the reader, for supporting this work—I hope it will benefit you for many years to come.